SHIPWRECKS
OF THE
NORTH-WEST COAST

David Cox, landscape painter, 1783–1859, spent some time sketching off the Lancashire coast.

SHIPWRECKS
OF THE
NORTH-WEST COAST

CATHERINE ROTHWELL

Great Marton Windmill – a landmark for ships out at sea, demolished in 1899-1900. Alongside is the Oxford Hotel and the old houses (left) are on the corner of Waterloo Road and Vicarage Lane, Marton.

First published 2009

The History Press
The Mill, Brimscombe Port
Stroud, Gloucestershire, GL5 2QG
www.thehistorypress.co.uk

British Library Cataloguing in Publication Data.
A catalogue record for this book is available from the British Library.

ISBN 978 0 7524 5307 1

Typesetting and origination by The History Press
Printed in Great Britain

CONTENTS

Acknowledgements

Special thanks must go to Ted Ramsey for providing the cover picture of the *Riverdance* wreck. Thanks to: Mr V. Baldwin, Poulton; British Transport Docks Board; The late Dr T. Blacklidge, Blackpool; Mr Dave Buckley, Fleetwood; Mr A. Coppin, Poulton; Mr B. Hammond Eardley, Fleetwood; *Evening Gazette*, Blackpool; *Fleetwood Chronicle*; Miss H. Geddes, Lancaster; The late Mr F. Graham, Poulton; Mrs, B. Hockey, Blackpool; Peter Horsley Ltd, Fleetwood; Isle of Man Steam Packet Co.; Lancashire Library; *Lancashire Evening Post*, Preston; Lancaster City Museum; The late Skipper Henry Leadbetter, Ramsey, Isle of Man; Mr Tony Lees, Carleton; Mr. H. Nickson, Poulton; Nostalgia Unlimited, Cleveleys; Mr R.G. Owens, Clwyd; Receiver of Wrecks, Heysham and Lancaster; Mr R. Roskell, Poulton; Royal National Mission for Deep Sea Fishermen; Mr R.G. Shepherd, Glasson Dock; Mr Ralph Smedley, Anchorsholme; St Andrew's Church, Cleveleys; Mr D.B. Timms, Lytham; Mr W.D. Trivess, Meonstoke; Mrs Dorothy Walker, Fleetwood; Mr F. Williams, Padgate; Mr R. Willoughby, Receiver of Wrecks, Fleetwood; Ashtons, Printers, Fleetwood; Atkinson Art Gallery, Southport; Mr R. Baxter, Fleetwood; The Late Dr Blacklidge; *Blackpool Gazette and Herald* Ltd; Blackpool Central Library; Botanic Gardens Museum, Churchtown; British Transport Docks Board; Mr G.W. Burrows, Southport; Mr D. Buckle, Fleetwood; Mr S. Cordt, Manchester; Mr R. Dobson, Staining; Mr W.N. Dodds, Bridgwater; Mr B.H. Eardley, Fleetwood; Fleetwood Chronicle; Miss E. Geddes, Lancaster; .Mr E. Graham, Poulton-le-Fylde: *Lancashire Evening Post*; Mr D. Hearn, Fleetwood; Lancashire Library, Preston; Lancashire Museum Service; Mr L.J. Hambling, Fleetwood; Lancaster City Museum; Mr A.J. Leather, Silverdale; Mr D. Leadbetter, Blackpool; Mr A. Lees, Carleton; Liverpool City Library; Lytham St Annes Library; Mrs D. Mann, London; Mr C. Martland, Fleetwood; Nostalgia Unlimited, Cleveleys; Mr Alan W.H. Pearsall, National Maritime Museum, Greenvvich; Pedlars Maze, Fleetwood; Peter Horsley, Fleetwood; Mr J.M. Pryce, Morecambe; Mr Patrick Ramsey, Cornwall; Mr W. Stammers, Liverpool; Mr Ralph Smedley, Cleveleys; Mr A.P. Tonks, Fleetwood; W.D. Trivess, Southampton; Mr R. Willoughby, Receiver of Wrecks; Mr 'Couch' Wright, Fleetwood; The Late Mr Jeff Wright; Mr K. Wilson; and finally, to three anonymous donors.

Right: Preston Town Hall in the nineteenth century.

Below: Fleetwood Docks in the nineteenth century, showing the railway station, Pharos Lighthouse and some moored ships. The wide central area used to be an archery ground.

Author Catherine Rothwell receives the highly commended Titus Wilson Award from Managing Director David Rigg for her book *Along the River Kent*, which featured some of the now vanished ports of Cumbria. (Courtesy of Ron Loomes)

Introduction

There was the sadness of a whole town whenever a ship was wrecked and men, known to so many people, were lost at sea. Such memories! The promenades thronged with people, before traffic congestion, evening strolls, the sighting of schools of porpoises, the regimental band playing, Solly's Pierrots, the fragrance of night-scented stock, the setting sun delineating the Isle of Man, well-lit ships on their nightly crossing of the Irish Sea and the short visits from sailors home from foreign lands with gifts of Turkish delight, lavender water, sticks of cinnamon, ginger, ivories and intricate wooden carvings from China...

Miss Elizabeth Coulson, born 19 August 1885, passed on to me many such memories, and I have tried to capture the essence of that exciting age of sea-voyaging which she describes so brilliantly. My grandfather vividly remembered the Mersey scene and the port of Fleetwood when scores of ships and fishing smacks were held up by head winds; forests of masts in dock and Pool etching a tracery like spiders' webs against the sky. After a prolonged spell of dirty weather, the wind could stand fair, and what a sight it was to witness all these outward-bounders making for the open sea. Along the coast were craft of every kind; brigantes, schooners, ketches calling at Sunderland Point, Arnside, Sandside, Milnthorpe, Lancaster, Lytham, Freckleton. There were fleets of sailing trawlers, fishing smacks and prawners with their dark-brown, freshly barked sails, each heading out to sea on every favourable tide and oh the joy and awe of boys when giant four-masters like the *Lawhill*, fresh from Canada, New Brunswick, arrived.

Marine artists were spoiled for choice, attempting to capture such an array of classic beauty, whilst experienced sea-dogs who had an eye for style could sum up a ship's points like shoremen would a racehorse. They said Harland & Wolff never designed an ugly ship. Raked masts were the hallmark of that yard, whilst Whitehaven was recognised for an appearance of strength and power in wood, so well expressed in such vessels as *Bowfell*, *Cambray* and *Burdwan*.

'The sea,' said Grandfather, 'had no time for the indecisive.' It bred virility, men of nerve, bone and character, because the true seaman had instinct. His was a calling. He knew the elements, pitted his wits against them, but had a healthy respect for fickleness of weather. In the days of the windjammers, the most famous of captains 'carried sail to the last', being capable of setting their top gallants and royals at first lull in the westerlies, and not reefing them until true seamanship recognised they had to. Reputations were lost and made on this faculty.

'Snugging down in time' was an art:

> The great four-mast barques could carry their sail through anything short of a hurricane but when the muslin had to come in it meant all hands for the greater part of a watch, the fore-course, on the rare occasions it had to be stowed, required all hands to a yard arm. If the skipper waited too long things began to go, and with really bad weather, even with the smartest work on clew and buntlines, sails would split. (Basil Lubbock)

It is plain that in the heart of a storm let rip in all its fury, skipper and crew were bound together in a precarious interdependence and could survive only if they worked together.

Sailors had to be skilled with palm and needle for making and mending in between squalls. The *Thunderbolt*, bound for Bombay from Liverpool, on one voyage had every sail blown away, but then she was skippered by a twenty year old.

Trailing a pulsing charisma from the days of sail, many are the stories that live on. How Captain Powles, born 1846, made a home of his ship. Tough in mind and body, he was a disciplinarian, while his wife, Mrs Powles, darned the men's socks, and in calm, sunny weather, crews could have music and sport. Whaling crews scratched designs on walrus tusks and windjammer sailors carved chunks of beef, five years old, black and

An interesting carving brought back by a north-western sailor, one of a crew who sailed to China in the 1870s. Some of the north-west sailing ships got as far as Shanghai and San Francisco, often going around Cape Horn.

From faraway places they brought back mementoes, this being a 'Pomegranate Old Man' of Chinese folklore, now over 100 years old.

Blackpool in the 1870s with fishing and pleasure boats on the beach. Bathing vans advertise Sunlight Soap and Jones's Sewing Machines.

hard as bog oak, to sell as curios. Captain Powles made thirty-two voyages, the longest from 6 May 1887 to 16 January 1889. He was well known in Liverpool as a sail carrier!

The Liverpool owners of the Waverley Line, J. Williamson and W.E.A. Milligan, named all their ships after Sir Walter Scott's novels. They had gloriously painted figureheads and on board were carved scenes from those romantic books. When *Marmion*, *Red Gauntlet* and *Talisman* docked, they pulled in the crowds. Thomas Horrocks, cotton merchant of Preston, had two fast schooners, each named *Devil* (it was said he did this in a fit of temper), voyaging from Liverpool or Preston to Newfoundland, then on with cod to the Mediterranean from where they returned with cargoes of raisins. *Devil II* was a lucky ship, but not so *Devil I*, ending her days wrecked on the bar of a West African river.

Being built in the summer added to a ship's value. The *Monsoon* which carried emigrants to Melbourne was sold for double her original price.

The *Maria* was made of 'golden pine, oak, iron and copper fastened'. Some of these beauties perished in their prime, sucked under in the grip of 'snorters'. Others, after years at sea, were burnt for their copper alone. Nostalgia for those magnificently built schooners, snows, barques and brigantines which once criss-crossed the sea-lanes has latterly led to 'wreck-trekking'.

This is a book mainly of shipwreck, storm and tempest, but perhaps what is best remembered are seagulls and flying spume, the creaming wake, that sublime blend of sea and sail summed up in a poem by John Masefield:

> Lay her before the wind
> Up with the canvas
> The wind begins to whistle
> Let her dance!

Whitehaven Docks.

Milnthorpe Fair.

1

Crucible of Storms

Sages and saints have gone down in history as performers of miraculous endurance. According to one of a plethora of legends, Saint Patrick, intent on bringing Christianity to our Northern shores, crossed the Irish Sea on a millstone. In another account he was shipwrecked in Morecambe Bay whilst bound on the same mission. Eight rock-hewn graves, worn by centuries of weather, lie close to the ruins of an early Saxon chapel dedicated to Saint Patrick, one of the most ancient in the country. The remains of its walls are 2½ft-thick, bonded by immensely strong mortar thought to have been made by burning seashells. Pervading all is the atmosphere and power of an omnipresent ocean, heightened by thoughts of the hag-bent thicket, once a Druid grove, which huddles as though shrugging off the wind and lies only a stone's throw distant.

From this impressive Heysham headland even on a calm, sky-blue day, gazing at what appears to be an infinite expanse can trigger vividly scenes of storm and tempest. No less impressive when the tide is out, the sand flats too seem infinite. Yet, with the sun shining on that mighty expanse – actually 120 square miles – they resemble a vast shield of burnished silver. A very good television programme termed them 'the wet Sahara', yet this wilderness trap – deadly without a guide – this nine-mile Over-Sands route across Morecambe Bay, drew the Romans, the Quakers and many before and after them as a short cut to the Furness Peninsula. To this day the traditional Over-Sands walk is slogged out; guide Cedric Robinson, who knows every inch of the way, a cheerful Moses with hundreds tagging on behind.

Sailors of old, although greatly daring, would never have attempted to cross the Irish Sea in winter, such a well-known fickle demon it was for spawning sudden storms. Saxon merchants who accomplished three safe voyages in their own ships were held in high esteem, automatically rising to the rank of Thane.

A great upsurge of the Irish Sea in 1555, one of at least ten such notable occasions on the north-west coast, submerged the village of Singleton Thorp, near Rossall. Adlingham-on-Walney was slowly but surely swept away. The fourteenth-century manor of Argameols, near Birkdale, along with ancient Aynesdale, vanished without trace, as did the Lords of Rossall lose the Manor of Chornet. Twenty-six other place names in the vicinity dropped out of use in land grants where previously they had mention. 'Ye lookers to ye Lord's wreck' are often referred to by successive Stewards in the Clifton Papers and the expression 'worn into the sea' crops up in chronicles again and again.

Country folk declare that once in every fifty years the sea comes back to claim its own, exacting a terrible vengeance. In my lifetime it has done just that – in 1927 and in 1977. Cartographers and geographers, whose maps corroborate a fluctuating coastline, for years mulled over and warned of the sea's encroachment. Camden, observing a huge sandbank stretching from Pile of Fouldray to the opposite side, thought that the shore must have 'once layout a great way westward into the ocean which the sea ceased not to slash and mangle until it swallowed the shore quite up...' and thereby made three bays, Morecambe Bay, 'the crooked sea' or 'bending shore' being one of the biggest in England. Rossall Grange, Pennystone, Gingle Hall, possibly the Roman *Portus Setantii*, the Horse Bank off Lytham, farms and fields where once cattle grazed, anchors, carcasses of ships, bottles, bones, leather, rope, earthenware, weapons and walls – all lie buried in plenty under the Irish Sea.

One of the loneliest places situated on the Bay must be that chosen by the Premonstratensian Order of the monks of Cockersand 800 years ago. Still secluded (at high tides the Cockerham and Thurnham roads can be impassable), in ancient days it was cut off by the impenetrable obstacle of the Moss. The Bishop of Saint Asaph would not venture, although ordered to visit, until he had hired an experienced man from Lancaster to ensure safe conduct for his party across the salt marsh. The boundary walls of the abbey of Saint Mary of the Marsh, flanking the sea, were in such danger from erosion by 1372 that Pope Gregory granted a Relaxation for twenty years to

Children enjoy donkey rides on Morecambe sands.

Building sandcastles on Blackpool Beach.

Opposite: Kents Bank and Morecambe Bay, from an old print.

penitents who gave money for repair. The waves not only endangered the monastery but embarrassed the inmates by washing the bones of dead brother monks from their graves, strewing them in profusion so that they whitened the beach. Years later, when a modern sea wall was built, stones from the abbey, besides finding their way into farm buildings, actually went into the sea defences. This would have pleased the canons for they were kind to seafarers, attending every night what must have been one of the first beacons on this coast. It guided sailors into the estuary of the Lune.

'Boreas is on the bluster' was the Lancashire coast saying when winds rose to gale force with such consequent havoc, and stories have passed into folklore to be handed down from generation to generation. In 1844 Thomas Bales or Birkenhead, a labourer, 'was blown over a precipice' by wind force, yet the only beacon to warn mariners of the dangers of approaching Ramsey Harbour was in that same year a gorse bush stuck on a pole at the end of the sunken pier head. Such sketchy arrangements prevailed that the making of a port at Fleetwood had been hailed as dire necessity. Ships had to find their way up the Ribble and Wyre and there were myriads of smaller calling places like Arnside, Milnthorpe, Ulverston, Sunderland Point and Freckleton. Experienced pilots gave evidence at the Court of Inquiry, quoting the old saying 'safe and easy as Wyre Water'. Captain Henry Mangles Denham said, 'The want of a harbour of refuge upon what is a lee shore nine months of the year is universally felt. The wrecks which have taken place off the Isle of Man from 1822 to 1841 exhibits the loss of 119 vessels, 122 lives and £207,902 worth of property.' His recommendations for charting Fleetwood Port were adopted rather than those of Captain Betcher some years before.

But the sea had its advantages to shore dwellers when unexpected 'gifts' were washed up. Edward I granted 'the wreck, wayfe and stray of Lytham' to his brother

Peel Castle: the twelfth-century castle drawn by T. Hearne, 1783, known on maps as the Pele or Pyle of Fouldrey (Pyle of Folder), was built on a small island between the east point of the Isle of Walney and the mainland. Ships could get to Furness only by passing through the narrow channel at high tide. The monks of Furness Abbey kept it in repair. By the sixteenth century it was much decayed but served as a landmark for mariners. A drawing was sent to Samuel Pepys when he was Secretary to the Admiralty in 1667, pointing out the vicinity as a dangerous place for ships.

The pier head, Fleetwood. Harbour of Refuge, 1836.

the Earl of Lancaster. Rich spoils of the sea were the subject of litigation and parley for many years. The Abbot of Cockersand allowed the Abbot of Cockerham, in 1230, every wreck that 'the turbulence of sea might cast ashore, when divine clemency sent aught'. In 'Pea soup year' the harvests failed but the boiling seas strewed bags of peas, providential for the Fylde. This good protein, eked out with cockles and fish, staved of starvation. 'Treacle winter' acted like manna from heaven but arrived in strong barrels. Beachcombers habitually gathered wooden flotsam which, once dried after its steeping in brine, made good kindling. Kitchen fires burned blue and friendly, often heating a mixture to keep sea boots watertight, which added somewhat to the smoky aroma of their thatched, squat cottage homes. The recipe consisted of one pint of boiled linseed oil, ½lb of mutton suet, 6oz of beeswax and 4oz of resin. Applied warm to leather, this 1845 concoction strongly reassured that you could stand in sea water and remain dry shod. Another recipe 'to clean black cloth stained with sea water' involved boiling fig leaves with milk. At least one man of the cloth, Parson Potter of Pilling, perhaps with the divine clemency clause in mind, was in the habit of wading into the sea alongside his flock to rescue anything that was going.

Between the Fylde coast and the Isle of Man a less respectable way of life than fishing flourished. Smuggling started in a small way, but between 1671 and 1765 was a thorn in the side of authority. One enthusiastic squire, Thomas Tyldesley of Fox Hall, Blackpool, had a schooner specially built for this illicit trade. Wardleys, where the renegade Captain Johnson's wherry put in, was a veritable smugglers' corner, and although the Customs Houses kept Seizing Records there was much that 'got away'. Daniel

Macinnes, a sailor found in possession of contraband whiskey, brought up before magistrate Giles Thornber at Poulton, was one of many in good, or rather bad, company. But smuggling, winked and connived at even by the Lord of the Manor, was considered a virtue compared with wrecking, stretches of the Liverpool coast being so notorious that the Constabulary reported 'Almost all the inhabitants along the coast are decidedly wreckers'. One sea captain said in 1825 he would rather be left to the mercy of the Hottentots than wrecked at Southport. Lanterns called 'Judas lights', carried by grazing beasts to lure and mislead ships, were the means they used. This practice was thunderously denounced in a sermon at St John's Church by William Thornber only two years after he had published his History of Blackpool. The vicar created a sensation and was looked at slightly askance as though having for once lost his sporting instincts, but as he was good with his fists, like Parson Potter, the sermon brooked no argument.

For every sixteen sailors dying in the 1840s, eleven died by drowning, or in wrecks. Graveyards near the sea tell their own pitiful story, not mentioning that frequently the cause was intemperance, although this frailty was scarcely to be wondered at, bearing in mind the mariner's hard and dangerous calling. His working life was finished at forty, even if he survived. Pinpointed in the old lifeboat houses are the areas where ships most frequently came to grief. Their records prove how busy the lifeboats were on such a stormy coast. Newspapers show a continuous thread of tempest and wreck, especially in the eighteenth and nineteenth centuries, but even with modern navigational aids and weather forecasts to warn of danger, there can still be trouble in Morecambe Bay. A glance at the chart reveals vast acres of sandbanks, causing shallow waters and a big tidal range, one of the most dramatic anywhere apart from the Brittany coast. Spring tides roar in with the speed of a cantering horse. Three rivers flow into these waters, which in times of high spate carry tree trunks and branches washed from their banks and capable of fouling propellers. Danger Patch, with its capricious mingling of currents, is well named. A calm, bright day can rapidly turn to squall.

In one small book it is possible to recount but few of these storms, with their resultant wrecks and damage, so I have attempted to set down chronologically the most interesting and human stories of all, placing them alongside events in history, some local, some national, storing in memory those untold ships that passed in the night with not a soul to witness a swift and terrible end.

2

Smuggling, Wrecking and Free For All

The Lancashire coast unfortunately is now almost denuded of boulders, the largest of which once had picturesque names and must have been a pretty sight. 'Old Mothers Head', to give one example off Blackpool, was reported in 1837 to be covered with pink sea anemones. Making the streets of Liverpool accounted for the huge stones at Rossall Point, a removal bitterly regretted later, as were the tons of 'golden gravel'. Such natural sea defences were dearly paid for in 1927 when the Great Flood swept an entire peninsula. Pennystone, Carlin and his Colts, Higher and Lower Gingle, Silkstone, Bear and Staff, the Coup, were familiar landmarks, passing into history as early as 1588 when Singleton Thorp was destroyed, inspiring the jingle: 'Penny stood, Carlin fled, Red Bank ran away'. According to tradition, Pennystone, now discernible as two rocks (the base split in 1923), stood alongside an inn whose patrons tied their horses to iron rings set in the wall whilst they drank their penny pots of ale. Excavation here in 1893 revealed the rafters of a large room, a doorpost, wall foundations and well-preserved tree trunks. Such great floods appear to have some link with the solar eclipses, occurring about every 200 years. In 1588 the sea never perceptibly ebbed, but flowed twice in twelve hours (as it did in November 1977), the level of the boiling spume being so high it shot over Thornton Marsh to meet the River Wyre. The tempestuous waves of that year helped to defeat the Spanish Armada, in which the north-west might well have played a vital part, for tradition also has it that staunch Roman Catholic Cardinal Allen, born at Rossall Grange, plotted with the King of Spain to invade England from Wyre mouth, giving rise to another couplet: 'If proud Spain would England win, At Min End she must come in', Min End being the entrance to the River Wyre.

Along the gale-beaten coasts of England floundered the unwieldy galleons. One drifting helplessly past the Isle of Man was blown towards Rossall Point and stranded by the tide. Squire Fleetwood hoped to capture the battered loot but was baulked

Entrance to the Wyre at low water. (G. Herdman lithograph)

of his prey as the weary Spaniards managed to re-float on the next tide, only to be wrecked shortly afterwards off Walney. How they must have wished they were back in sunny Spain. Two cannon balls, feebly fired as the dejected crew got off the sand-bank at Rossall, were kept as mementos at Rossall Hall for years. Nineteen galleons were cast up on the shores of Ireland, Scotland and Northern England after that rousing victory and the old-world atmosphere of Biggar, near Vickerstown, is enhanced by black oak beams in the Queen's Arms, said to have come from the timbers of the wrecked galleon. The Horse Bank of Lytham, destined in time to become a cemetery for ships, was then still in use as lush pasture, as it was well into the reign of James I. By the 1820s it was far out at sea. News of another Spanish ship in the north-west, again off Rossall Point, but this time a frigate, came in 1643. The *Saint Anne* of Dunkirk, blown off course while carrying troops for training in the Netherlands, came ashore near Wyre mouth, beaching at the ancient look-out station named Bergerode. Civil war rumours were running like fire in flax throughout Lancashire. Such red-hot news brought detachments of contending armies, each intent on claiming the prize although it did not concern either of them. Parliamentarian Major Sparrow had the advantage but ceded to Royalist Lord Derby who set fire to the ship, and as it burned heavy guns fell through the decks. The Parliamentarians were said to recover all of these later on, but in 1962 a scrap metal firm dredged up and disposed of, at a good

The *Saint Anne*, drawn by Tony Lee.

price, a fine bronze cannon (possibly from the *Saint Anne*). The Spanish gentry were diplomatically returned via London, but the poor crew were driven off to fend for themselves, some pushing south, others perishing from cold and starvation. The ones taken pity on by farming families in Rossall have dark-haired, dark-eyed descendants still around.

In 1660 a shipwreck off Pilling near where Fluke Hall now stands is said to have resulted in two survivors scrambling exhausted ashore, to be succoured by a poor family who had scarcely enough for their own needs. None realised that the mariners carried in their bodies the dreaded plague, and within a week every occupant of that house was dead. For their own preservation villagers put it to the flame, laying two gravestones in memory on the shore. Worn now totally indecipherable by sea action, the crude inscription 'C. Dickonson Margaret His Wife Burid 1660' was still visible in 1872. A farmer building a barn once tried to utilise them but each morning, so the story goes, the stones had been carried back. Fearing them bewitched, he wisely let them lie to brave out the centuries in peace.

1702 and 1703 were storm years all round the coasts. The Royal Navy lost thirteen ships in rough waters, a sinister number to those most superstitious of all people – sailors. William Stout, a Lancashire merchant, tells of a rattling adventure when 'our ship the Employment met with a French ship... who made a prize of her'. John Gardner, the brave Master, tried to bargain, but the French stripped the crew even of their clothing so that they became too weak to work the ship. Gardner agreed to stand as surety for £1,000 and remained with his captors whilst the mate, William Barrow, an inexperienced man in charge of a sickly crew, had the task of steering *Employment* to land. Embayed off Wales, they made with difficulty to the Isle of Man, missed their course, mistook Rossall Mill for Walney Mill and finally ran under the Red Banks at Bispham early in August 1702. The crew got ashore and managed to send word to Customs before the ravening natives could lighten the ship. Horses and carts came from Lancaster with empty casks in which to put the damaged sugar, and as quickly as possible all that could be saved was hurried off – 'the sugar into Squire Fleetwood's barn at Rossall, the old saffron-walled wreck barn, the cotton wool into Bispham Chapel'. They got the carpenters to work, but such a storm came with the rising tides that it beat the *Employment* to pieces. The cotton wool was sent to Manchester and sold for £200. It is to be hoped that John Gardner, very much a Rossall sea-faring name, was ransomed. That trip from Barbados was the last the *Employment*, built at Warton, ever made.

In 1709 'Lookers to Ye Lord's Wreck', Thomas Hall, George Brown, Thomas Hankinson and Richard Graddell developed hawks' eyes and ears on behalf of Squire Clifton. There were more storms and resultant reports of 'infamous wretches plundering what the elements had spared'. Tempests in 1717 demolished 175 houses in Lytham and flooded 7,000 acres, leaving a trail of destruction as far back as Cockerham. Such rising of the waters had led to the apocryphal story that Noah's Ark, in passing over Preesall Hill, left scratches on its side. Small wonder stories were passed down the generations when corn, hay, turf, household goods – everything those poor souls had – was swept away. They saved themselves by hanging on to the lofts of their thatched cottages, and when the waters subsided, for months afterwards they fell asleep gazing at the stars through roofless dwellings. The Lytham Charities resulted from a 'dreadful inundation of the sea' in December 1719 when, 'at the change of moon and height of the Spring tide, ramparts and sea fences were destroyed'. Petitions for help were presented not only by Lytham but by the inhabitants of North Meols, Hesketh-cum-Becconsall, Tarleton, Martin Mere, Pilling, Cockerham and Ince Blundell. 6,600 acres were inundated and the sum claimed for damages was £10,227.

In these coastal storms amongst those to suffer badly were the salt wellers. Peter Townley of Cockerham spoke of his ruin at the quarter sessions in 1701. He and his

Lytham Custom House was probably built to keep down smuggling on the Fylde coast, or as a watch tower against invasion. Lytham was a port long before Preston, old wharves being not far from the Custom House. The only clue to its date of erection was 1850, on a fall pipe on the south wall.

two sons had rented and worked a saltcote which the storm wrecked (as it did again in 1720), destroying equipment and the precious, purified salt. For one and a half hours the tide kept its height, sweeping up river mouths and bringing down bridges, such as that over the Cocker.

The storm of 29 July 1768, accompanied by thunder, lightning and torrential rain, drove the bowsprit of the Liverpool ship *Wheel of Fortune* through the middle window of a house at the bottom of James Street. The Minutes of the Lancaster Port Commissioners show that on 15 January 1770 the brig *Hamilton*, commanded by Captain Parkinson, damaged the outperch in foul weather to the tune of £10-6-4¾, half of which had to be paid by Captain Parkinson himself. In the same year that seven seamen returned to Liverpool after twelve months' slavery on the Barbary Coast, 1773, the Kitty Grimshaw was lost at the Rock. Interest turned to the Ribble in 1774 when the Annual Register recorded that on 24 December the river stood still for three miles of its expanse. There was no water except in deep places but after five hours once more the current flowed strongly. It happened again on 8 March 1821, vagaries coinciding with wild weather and winds of such velocity that a man passing over a bridge near Preston on 28 August 1736 saw two flights of birds meet with a force that felled 180 of them; whereupon this opportunist gathered them up for sale that day in the town's market.

The Red Banks or cliffs at Bipsham were washed into the sea over the ages, but the bases of these cliffs are still to be found. The photograph shows an erratic ice age boulder washed up from one of the ancient 'red banks' and made into a sundial outside Norbreck Hotel.

Aided by dark, moonless nights and bad weather, the 'great fraudulent trade' of smuggling near Ribble and Wyrewater was reported from Liverpool on 22 February 1740 to the Board of Commissioners as generally coming from the 'Isleman'. One large wherry belonged to a noted smuggler called Knight, until his gang was broken up, after which Captain Johnson did most of the running. Of 16-tons burthen, with a ten-man crew, they used a method which lent itself to the Lancashire coast. The shallow-draughted wherries came on the turn of the tide, slipping the casks overboard at a pre-determined place. A shore party would come down to recover them on the ebb and, if disturbed, would bury them in sand. Riding officers tried to keep look-out by covering the districts of the ports on horseback, but it was a thankless and difficult task, so as revenue was at hazard, in 1730 a separate Tide Surveyor was appointed by Lancaster to be stationed at Sunderland Point 'where there is a lawfullkey and stone-houses'. The River Lune was silting and new landing places were needed, but the authorities, fearing more illicit approaches, ordered that goods must be put on board lighters and 'brought to keys under the care of trusty Tidesmen'. Seizing Records were kept at the Custom Houses but, aided by the elements, illicit trade was roaring between the years 1671 and 1765.

Wardleys, on the Wyre, was reported to have a smuggler's ghost which haunted the place, particularly the old warehouses, in the days when commerce with the Baltic and West Indies was brisk. The belts of sand dunes that then existed were good hiding places for casks, the River Wyre a convenient escape route. Smugglers were busy at Knott End, Staynall, the Gynn and South Blackpool, meeting Irish vessels out at sea and winging off to the Starr Hills to land spirits hidden under fish, although Captain Trafford's mounted dragoons were stationed at Blackpool to prevent this from happening. A King's Cutter pursued a sloop conveying contraband goods to the coast under cover of a gale in 1780, and the smuggler, to save his skin, ran his vessel ashore not far from Lytham.

In 1775 the Traver Indiaman, richly laden with silks and lace, was struck during a storm by a vessel commanded by Captain Hallowell. She sank immediately, all on board perishing except one seaman who, at the point of impact, desperately leapt on board the other ship. The wreck of the Traver was a great temptation, but the Lord of the Manor, who had rights over the wreck of the sea, made examples or plunderers in order to deter others. Notwithstanding his severity, items were buried, to be recovered later. Traver lace decorated the caps and gowns of Fylde beauties for many years, carefully removed from old garments to adorn new. Two beautiful blue and white Chinese vases were recovered from the sea and taken to Rossall Hall. They

Customs House, Arnside.

Nether Bridge, Kendal.

Collapsed chimney at Moss Bay, Workington, 1913.

now reside at Meols Hall, Churchtown, receptacles for fragrant pot pourri from the rose gardens.

Nine sailors died in 1787 after attempting to reach land at Rossall Point. After the storm they were found with their small boat lying beside them; probably with no immediate assistance on hand they died of exposure after cheating the sea.

There is, however, evidence from Glazebrook's list of ships wrecked and saved during the period 1786–1824 that men along the coast were engaged in rescuing poor unfortunates, even though they gained no reward. The North Meols boatmen in 1816 (a particularly bad year, for there were nine ships lost and several others damaged off the Southport coast) gave valiant assistance, one pilot steering an Irish brigantine with a cargo of linen to safety, but all he received was 'raw pork and cold water'. Others preferred to wait until the ship was beyond hope, although they knew crew and cargo were in danger. An instance of this occurred in 1825, witnessed by an outraged visitor to Southport who subsequently wrote to the Liverpool press about such scandalous inhumanity. In 1786 Register Books for merchant shipping were begun under Lord Liverpool's Registry Act at Liverpool, Preston and Lancaster to cover the Lancaster Customs area, and they show 200 ships totalling 25,000 tons (Liverpool), twenty-four ships totalling 1,430 tons (Preston) and forty-six ships at Lancaster. On 20 March 1793 a man o' war brig, the *Pelican*, foundered in the Mersey, drowning seventy persons. An old 28-pounder gun

A Chinese pagoda, designed by Sir Decimus Burton on the Mount of Fleetwood. It was replaced some years later by the Mount Pavillion. (The Mount was the highest in a chain of sand hills.)

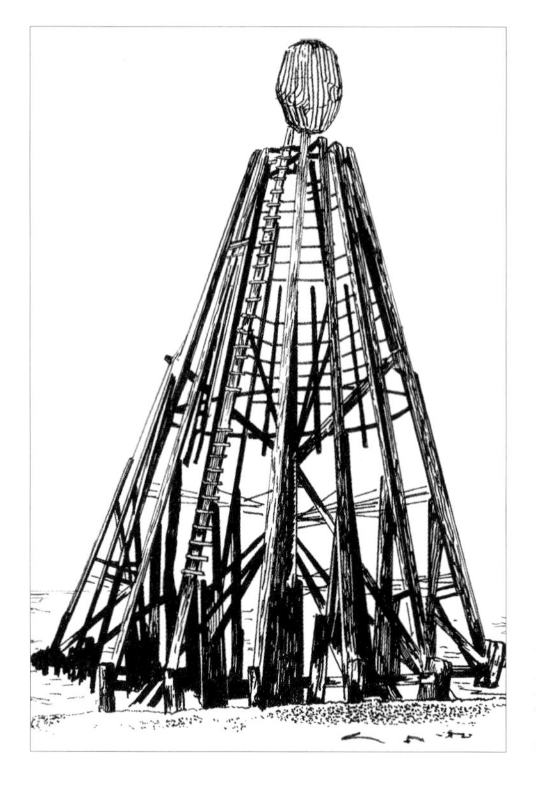

Pen drawing by my late brother John Charles Houghton of the Rossall Landmark (shown below), an early beacon to guide ships, built in 1740, and later washed away.

found on 20 September 1859 was supposedly from the *Pelican*. On 3 May 1793 there blew up a dreadful gale, which turned over the *William Kitchen* (a Frodsham market boat, approaching Liverpool), sank several flats in the river and drowned seventeen people. A perfect hurricane on 2 February 1794 filled the River Mersey with wreckage and destroyed a wooden mill that had weathered many previous gales.

The amount of wreck timber available was instanced by William 'Duke' Sutton who used it to construct a bathing house for Churchtown swimmers and visitors. Many old wrecks in the Fylde supplied farm gateposts from their masts and timbers. At one time people could recall the name of the wreck from which the gates were derived.

A survey of the coasts and rivers of the port of Lancaster was made in August 1799 by a committee of six masters of vessels appointed at the request of the Commissioners to survey the area with a view to providing 'greater safety than at present'. The provision of a landmark at Rossall Point had been decided on 12 June 1766, but the model made by Mr Richard Walker, costing £137, they reckoned was too expensive. Bold Fleetwood Hesketh had granted leave to fix the landmark for *2/6d* per annum ground rent. It was completed on 17 June 1767, but Minutes show that it had to be replaced or repaired more than once. In less than a year rough seas had reduced it to a shattered condition and in 1797 the Rossall Point structure was again a source of trouble.

New buildings in Liverpool were blown down and houses unroofed on 12 November 1799 by a hurricane which wrecked the *Ellis* and the *Souter* in Bottle Bay. The *Hope* and *Belfast* were lost with all hands, and so the century ended on a clarion note, the year lovingly known in Blackpool as 'Pea Soup'.

3

'NOW VOYAGER, SAIL THOU FORTH...'

– OLIVE HIGGINS PROUTY

'Now the anticipating heart,
  Longs for the pilgrimage to start.'

The anticipating heart' may well be forgiven for painting too rosy a picture with thoughts of a new country and a new life ahead, but a sea voyage for the rank and file on emigrant ships was no light undertaking. Small wonder that those who survived and did indeed make landfall, kissed the ground as they stepped ashore, like the Pilgrim Fathers or the New World aspirants of the *Seven Sisters* masted barque that sailed from Skippool and was built there at the ancient port of Poulton-le-Fylde.

Robert Louis Stevenson in his book *The Amateur Emigrant* describes conditions well. 'To descend on an empty stomach into Steerage was an adventure that required some nerve. The stench was atrocious. It tasted in the throat like some horrible kind of cheese – so many people worming themselves into their clothes.'

The beginning of the new century witnessed a riot by Liverpool sailors over their appallingly low wages, and as if to underline the dangers, on 21 January 1802 there occurred another hurricane off the Lancashire coast. The *Peggy of Greenock* smashed on the rocks near the Wishing Gate, Liverpool, only fifty yards from the shore, drowning twelve. Tides rose 6ft higher than calculated in the tide tables, and a packet boat from Blackpool was wrecked. It being a freezing storm, only three out of eighteen got ashore to survive the experience. The sails of Cockerham Mill whirled so madly that sparks set it alight, and as it burned fragments fell onto the thatch of two cottages and a barn, all of which were razed to the ground. The wind did great damage, blowing down the Oversands Coach in Morecambe Bay as soon as it attempted the crossing. Three passengers inside were badly shaken but otherwise unhurt. People were becoming more

Port St Mary, Isle of Man, 1895. The Isle of Man Steam Packet vessels steamed thousands of miles, but had a number of mishaps along the way. For example, *Peel Castle* ran aground on 7 June 1924, until the *Fenella* (1881) finally towed her clear of the sandbanks off Douglas.

lifeboat-conscious. On 22 October 1802 a new one was paraded through the streets of Lancaster and sent to Liverpool on a large wagon for passage to the Isle of Man. It was presented to the island by the Duke of Athol, who owned much of Douglas. On 7 October 1808 the *Lancaster Guardian* reported 'many disasters amongst the shipping along the coast'. This was possibly the year when the *Howard* was wrecked off Southport with a cargo of cotton, whitening the shore for miles. She had, most unusually, not a woman but a gilt lion as a figurehead, which later graced a shop in Chapel Street, Southport, until it vanished from the scene. Hand-carved, it had the dignity and rareness which seem to sit naturally on all old things made by man.

From Lancaster between 1811 and 1816 many sailings were being made to the West Indies for cocoa, rum, sugar and cotton, meeting not only storms but enemy action. Captain Greenwood of Lancaster was presented by Lloyds Underwriters with a piece of plate valued at 100 guineas for achieving thirty-two successful voyages and for having (in the *William Ashton* of Lancaster, mounting sixteen 9-pounders and with twenty-five men) beaten off a French corvette of eighteen 18-pounders and 125 men. Bold Fleetwood Hesketh of Rossall Hall wrote to his cousin in 1814: 'I am sure you will be sorry to hear that I have suffered very severely by the late storms. My fleet is all blown up on Cartmell Sands'. The following year a ghostly brig drifted onto the beach at Blackpool, the only living thing on board being the ship's cat, which was taken lovingly to land by the villagers and lived amongst them like a lord ever after. About the same time some Blackpool fishermen alighted on a hoard of porter, supposedly casks lost on the sandbanks from a wreck, or perhaps buried to be recovered at a later date! Old salts in the district, with amazing intuition, seemed to know all about it and declared it was thirty years ago. Notwithstanding its long immersion, sampling at Simpson's Hotel proved it to be in excellent condition. The year 1816 washed up at South Shore, Blackpool, lard, flour and a bounteous supply of bacon. Despite threats from the Customs House Officers to prosecute all persons plundering the wrecks, it remained an irresistible local sport. When a Mr Butcher of Blackpool commenced building Raikes Hall, his neighbours wondered where he got the money from until they recalled his constant visits to the shore. It was rumoured that he had discovered the wealth on the *Three Sisters*, a ship lost in an 1820s storm, and he gained the reputation of being a generous man. 1821 saw the highest tide for twenty years, breaching the new embankment at Oldcliffe and inundating St George's Quay, Lancaster. Ships in Bootle Bay were wrecked by the 1823 hurricane on 3 December which caused more serious accidents than at any time since 1560 when the Haven (beginning of Liverpool) was utterly destroyed. Equinoctial gales were particularly violent. Off the Isle of Man, where coasts were notorious, there occurred in 1824 wrecks at Langness, Spanish Head (with its tradition of drifting Spanish warships), Poolvash (the Bay of Death) and Douglas Head. One such

The old Gynn Inn, on the cliffs at Blackpool, where many a smuggling and wrecking story was recounted over the pewter pots. Artist P.C. Miller drew an impression early in the twentieth century of the wreck of a Scottish sloop whose crew were saved in 1833 by making for the creek by the Gynn Inn, guided by a lighted candle in one of the windows. It was placed there by the landlord's daughter, and the romantic story has it that she later married the captain of the wrecked ship.

The building of the Preston and Wyre Railway was almost defeated by the crossing of Kirkscar Bay. Tons of Overton stone were washed away by storms in 1838, and eventually a timber trestle was used to carry the line but it sufficed for only a few years, so great was the strength of the tides.

Opposite: A 1922 painting by C. Travis, of a famous wreck in 1833, saved by the light in the Gynn Inn.

storm destroyed 100 fishing boats and claimed 132 lives. With this shocking event in mind, Sir William Hillary built the Tower of Refuge on Connister Rock, which over the ensuing years was to save 300. 1824 also recorded the wrecking of the sloop *Fanny* of Blackpool, with her cargo of black, blue and red cloth flung to the waves. Inevitably 'Fanny' coats to warm the populace appeared when bolts of cloth had been given sufficient time to dry out. Some remembered it as 'red petticoat year'.

Gales wrought ever-changing patterns in the sandhills all along the Lancashire coast. With mouths swathed and heads down, villagers battled through sandstorms. Like the monuments of Egypt that had lain under the shining sands of the desert, the amazing sight of the remains of seven wrecks of wooden vessels from 200-250 tons were revealed, lying in a line at Formby where they had probably beached. Two days later they were covered up again by gales once more shifting and reshaping the sandhills. Similarly the 'lost farm' at Ainsdale, associated with an incident in the 1745 rebellion, was gradually covered by blowing sand. Part was still visible in 1824 but nothing was to be seen of it by 1840.

The wreck of the brig *James and Frederick*, which threw Lytham into turmoil, took place on Tuesday 18 January 1825. Laden with corn and butter from Port Patrick and bound for Liverpool, after experiencing heavy gales of wind that sent 'greybeards' sweeping and crashing over the lee rails, on Tuesday at 4 a.m. she sprang a leak. Men worked frenziedly at the pumps, using every means in their power, but seas gained so much that the vessel became waterlogged and unmanageable. At 4 p.m. she stuck on the south side of Horse Bank. Crews of Southport fishermen, perceiving the crew's danger, set out in two boats and, after much buffeting, they managed to get alongside the brig and bring off the whole crew. There is no doubt that prompt action from the Southport men saved lives. The brig's longboat being stoved in, the sailors were attempting to make and set forth in a raft, which would surely have been disastrous with such high seas running. The Preston newspaper later reported: 'the brig is a total wreck... four puncheons of bread were found at Sea Dyke, presumably part of the ship's stores'.

A two-day storm commencing on 29 November 1833 did great mischief. Pilot boat No.1, *Good Intent*, was wrecked at Formby, drowning thirteen, but one of the worst storms ever remembered occurred on 31 December. For five hours the wind blew at hurricane force. Recorded at Liverpool, the tide rose to a height never known before – from 17ft 5in to 26ft, flooding cellars and inundating streets. The grounds of Rossall Hall were so devastated they never recovered; outbuildings were ruined; sheep, cattle, deer and wildlife perished. Rats were seen to cling to the backs of sheep in efforts to save themselves, a repetition of the summer storm of 11 June when eleven wrecks strewed the coast. One famous story, already reported on page 33, tells how a Scottish schooner was saved on that occasion by steering for a light placed in a window of the Gynn Inn whose landlord, Mr Snape, boasted that the storm could never shift his tavern on the cliffs. It did, however, flood his cellars. That Sunday the Reverend Thornber's text com-

The end of a long sea voyage from Liverpool. Weary passengers wait to disembark in the 1800s.

menced 'When he saw the wind boisterous he was afraid'. In thankfulness the rescued crew attended St John's Church, Blackpool, where the ship's mate was presented with an inscribed bible. Over the ensuing week wrecks floated past Blackpool – a sorry sight. The storm-tossed 1800s led to an inquiry in 1834 about the safety of mariners and the jeopardised commercial interests of the whole country. 'Much unnecessary danger has arisen to vessels navigating this coast from the want of a lighthouse and the erection of distinctive marks at the entrance into the Ribble'. Improved Ribble navigation was called for as it was no uncommon thing, reported historian Edward Baines in 1836, for ships bound for Liverpool to overshoot the Mersey when a brisk southerly wind was behind them and to sail by mistake up the Ribble with its dreaded sandbanks, which meant one thing to ships' masters: 'Abandon hope all ye who enter here'. But the toll continued. On 7 April 1838 the Liverpool ship *Athabaska*, bound for Quebec, was lost in a gale, all aboard perishing. 1839: 'a terrific and most destructive hurricane on the sixth of January with destruction of property and very great loss of life'. On the 15th, Sir Peter Hesketh Fleetwood wrote to his brother the Reverend Charles Hesketh, at Southport, 'How thankful I should be that the banks at Rossall did not suffer'. The Hesketh Fleetwoods spent a fortune on sea defences but the 1833 gale caused the sandstone blocks of a wall thought to be impregnable, the boast of its contrivers, to be tossed like matchboxes.

Small wonder that a lucrative 'trade in spoiling wrecks' burgeoned amongst the grain and timber ships of those years. Local lads, like jackals, arrived with carts and

In 1839 the *Crusader*, 584 tons, bound for Bombay from Liverpool with £60,000 worth of silks and carrying Government dispatches, grounded on North Bank, opposite the Starr Hills. The captain and crew got ashore in two boats by pouring oil on the troubled seas to calm them. Four boats which left Liverpool on the same day were also lost, their sails torn to shreds, although they were 'as thick as a bull's ear'. Drawing by Tony Lees.

stripped any ship caught by tides and storm-driven into shallow waters, before any attempt at salvage could be made by the owners.

So severe was the 1839 storm it is deserving of special mention. The hurricane of Sunday and Monday, 6 and 7 January, spread damage over a wide area inland. Mr and Mrs Dobson of the Royal Oak Inn, Garstang, fearing for one of their chimneys, left the bedroom just in time to avoid half a ton of bricks and rubble which smashed their bed. Buildings were blown down at Catterall Hall, Barnacre, the Green Man, Myerscough and a huge tree uprooted at Nateby Hall. The general unroofing of houses and falling of chimneys attendant upon the hurricane struck terror. Although doors were secured by bolts, locks and iron chains, the wind burst them in; thatch and slate littered the fields and hedges, and miles inland were covered with salt particles so thick they resembled hoarfrost. Thatch was very scarce when repairs got underway and for a time Starr grass was used instead and found to be an excellent substitute, as birds and rats did not favour it so much. However, removal of Starr grass caused more trouble with blowing sands.

Meanwhile, out at sea, that great beauty *Crusader* was doomed. A large, full-rigged East Indiaman sheathed in copper, she carried a cargo worth a fortune – £100,000, only part of which was recovered. Ever afterwards the place where she sank was known as Crusader Bank. In 1867 a shifting of sandbanks caused more cargo to erupt and for years a white jug from the *Crusader* was on view at Castle Inn, Blackpool. All the crew were saved and looked after at the Britannia Inn, South Shore. Hogsheads of tobacco floated from the '95 wrecked *Favourite*, and other casualties were the *Anne Paley*, *Denis Cany* and *Arion Davies*. The 'north-west' entrance buoy of the Ribble broke adrift, coming ashore at Red Sank, Bispham. Amongst the variety of goods cast up were elephants' teeth.

Seafowl were picked up exhausted along the Lancashire shoreline, such was the length of the raging storm. The distress of families who had lost husbands, brothers and fathers was made more pathetic as in some cases it was not the first bereavement caused by the sea. A certain widow Walmsley of Liverpool lost her husband by the upsetting of the lighthouse boat, and in 1839 her brother was drowned in a pilot boat. Widow Roberts, for whom a subscription was raised in 1841, 'was enabled to support herself by a mangle purchased for her'. The bodies of unknown sailors were buried by the benevolence of the local squire, who paid 6/8*d* each. It was savage justice, but

Emigrants bound for America, *c.*1900.

Wyre Light, a beacon since 1840, when it appeared as one of the most important features of the harbour improvements recommended by Captain Henry Mangles Denham, has finally been extinguished after 140 years' service.

An engraving was made from this drawing for Bradshaw's *Manchester Journal* of 1839, showing the imposing crescent-shaped North Eustan Hotel and the Lower Lighthouse, both designed by architect Decimus Burton. The lighthouse, with tall Pharos Light and Wyre Light at the foot of the river where ships turned, enabled mariners to steer a course to port by aligning the lights one above the other. This made Fleetwood Harbour the safest on the north-west coast.

when starting up house again, what better to make furniture from than the timber salvaged from wrecks? Back in the mists of time, where legend fuses with fact, it was just such a storm as that of 1839 that destroyed the ancient forest of Amounderness, the remains of which, laid in one direction, can still be seen at the lowest tides of the year off Fleetwood and Blackpool.

Destruction of life and property in Liverpool was great. The *Brighton*, from Bombay, was wrecked near Middle Patch Buoy; fourteen of her crew drowned in attempting to reach shore on a raft. *Harvest Home* foundered on Mad Wharf, some of her crew having taken refuge in the rigging for forty hours. Fifty-five people were saved out of 108 from the *Lochwoods*, an emigrant ship; twenty-three from the *St Andrew* and twenty-six from the *Pennsylvania* (the last two named were bound for New York with valuable cargoes). Liverpool Humane Society put up £5,000 for the relief of their distressed, but the dwellers in the Fylde were not so fortunate.

Scarcely recovered from 1839, 1840 came in like a lion. The crew and passengers of the barque *Corsair*, sailing from Halifax to Liverpool, were saved by the steam tug *President*, but the vessel was wrecked. That year the harbour improvements at Fleetwood involved the skilful erection of the Screw Pile Lighthouse, designed by the blind engineer Alexander Mitchell, achieved in just two months. It was the first of its kind to be lit, which aroused so much interest that a model was sent to London for experts to examine. The new port was praised as being approachable for eighteen hours out of twenty-four, with no obstructions, lighted by night and beaconed by day, 'a refuge to which, when crippled and driven by westerly and north-westerly gales, mariners can find shelter and safety at half-tide at a jump, as it were, from ocean water'. In contrast, the Ribble offered twenty miles of shallows and sandbanks; the Lune twelve miles of similar impediments. Captain Henry Mangles Denham, in charge of the harbour improvements, was full of praise for this port of refuge on a stormy coast.

The early 1840s were years of bickering rivalry between the ports of Preston and Fleetwood, which did not aid situations at sea. Ecclesiastical oratory waxed lyrical, with extravagant Victorian phrases about 'briny avalanches, ever restless but never weary; the vast Leviathan ploughed by a thousand keels'; and high-sounding paradoxes about the ebbing and flowing sea analogous with the storms of human life were no more helpful in practical ways. Sailors, between voyages, spent much of their time in a state of intoxication, blotting out thoughts of the next. 'A halo of shame hung over two seamen who rolled out of a church pew just as the Reverend Gentleman was about to bestow a blessing'. About the same time, in Fleetwood, on board the *Prince of Wales*, casks labelled as fresh meat bound for Bolton were found to contain whiskey.

The steamer *William Huskisson*, which belonged to the City of Dublin Co., foundered whilst on a voyage from Dublin to Liverpool in mid-channel on 11 January

1840. Fortunately the steamer *Huddersfield*, outward-bound from Liverpool, discovered the distressed vessel, by which time the water had risen to such a height that it had put out the engine fires. The captain of the *Huddersfield* came swiftly alongside though the sea was so violent the vessels fouled each other. In their terror some passengers leapt into the sea and were drowned, but ninety-four crew and passengers were taken off. The captain of the *Huddersfield* was reluctantly forced to leave six passengers on the wreck as inaccessible, for to remain was to risk the lives of all on board and the safety of his ship. When the *Huddersfield* moved off, water was rising so rapidly that the *William Huskisson* vanished within forty minutes.

'Now Voyager, sail thou forth to seek and find...' Thousands of emigrants took this advice, thinking that neither the oceans nor the unknown that beckoned could be worse than the famines they had already endured, but the cruel sea hungered after many an emigrant ship. The *Governor Fenner*, property of Messrs Andrews Brothers & Co. of New York, was a wooden sailing vessel of 500-tons burden. She left the Mersey at noon on Friday 18 February 1841 with a large cargo of manufactured dry goods and many passengers, mainly Irish. As the wind was fresh the ship was travelling under double-reefed topsails when suddenly a steamer was sighted on the larboard. The captain hastily ordered the helm to be put hard to port to give as wide a berth as possible, but the fast-approaching steamer struck amidships with such force that sinking of one or the other or even both seemed inevitable. All passengers and crew, apart from the watch on deck, were in their berths. 'For God's sake, save yourselves, the ship is sinking,' cried the Captain of the *Governor Fenner*, calling the watch forward, but in confusion they ran aft, cutting of their only chance. Mate and captain left together, the only ones to be saved, forced to give up all hope of helping others as their ship sank in about one minute, taking with her all passengers and sixteen crew, amounting in all to 122 souls. The mate's account tallied with the captain's. There was no time to lower a boat. In despair, the mate, whose wife was amongst the lost, somehow got into the rigging and onto the foreyard which was crossing the steamer. From here he dropped down to safety amongst some sheep, with the awful cries of the watch on the starboard deck of the stricken *Governor Fenner* ringing in his ears: 'For God Almighty's sake save us.'

The steamer *Nottingham*, which finally berthed in Clarence Dock, was visited by hundreds of curious sightseers, and Liverpool was plunged into sorrow after this tragedy.

Less than a month later, on 11 March 1841, the steamship *President* left New York for Liverpool, but failed to arrive. The many passengers on board included Tyrane Power, a popular comedian, a son of the Duke of Richmond and other distinguished people. Ship after ship arrived in the port without bringing any news, so hope faded and, reluctantly, the public accepted that the steamer had gone down with all hands. *The Times* of 14 May printed a long poem about the tragedy, its last lines reading, 'man cannot urge the barque, or guide the sailor or force the quivering helm'.

STAR

EX-ROYAL MAIL LINE OF

AUSTRALIAN PACKETS.

These Magnificent Clippers, which have been so long and successfully employed in the conveyance of Her Majesty's Mails between Liverpool and the Australian Colonies, are despatched from

LIVERPOOL TO MELBOURNE,

On the 20th and 27th of every Month,

FORWARDING PASSENGERS, BY STEAM, AT THROUGH RATES, TO

GEELONG, SYDNEY, HOBART TOWN, LAUNCESTON,

AND ALL PARTS OF AUSTRALIA.

STEAM IS TAKEN TO CLEAR THE CHANNEL, IF NECESSARY.

RED JACKET, O'Halloran . .	4,500	SHALIMAR, I. R. Brown . . .	3,500
WHITE STAR, — Kerr . . .	5,000	ARABIAN, W. Balmano	2,500
GOLDEN ERA, H. A. Brown .	3,500	ANNIE WILSON, — Duckett.	3,500
MERMAID, Devey	3,200	TITAN, — Sears	5,000

The Ships of this Line are known to the World as the LARGEST and FASTEST afloat, and are fitted up regardless of expense, to suit the various means of every class of Emigrants. From the Saloon to the Steerage every article of dietary is put on board under the careful inspection of Her Majesty's Officers of Emigration, who likewise superintend the proper disposal of the necessary light and ventilation. The Saloons are elegant and roomy. The Second Cabins are fitted up with unusual care, and Passengers in this class have Stewards appointed to wait on them. The Intermediate and Steerage berths are exceedingly lofty, and the sexes are thoroughly separated. A properly qualified Surgeon is attached to each Ship.

RATES OF PASSAGE.

Saloon	£45 to £60
Second Cabin	£25 to £30
Intermediate, according to Rooms . .	£17 to £20
Steerage	£14

As Conveyances for Fine Goods, these Ships have long had a preference, having uniformly discharged their cargoes in first-rate order, and goods sent out by them can be Insured at the Lowest Rates of the day. For particulars of Freight or Passage, apply to the Owners,

H. T. WILSON & CHAMBERS,

21, WATER STREET, LIVERPOOL.

Agents in Melbourne . . . . H. T. WILSON & Co., 41, King Street.

November gales in 1844 sank the fishing smack *Jane and Lenny* of Port St Mary, manned only by the captain and one sailor. Ten poor passengers had sought transit, being unable to afford the regular packet boat. A sudden hurricane carried away the sails and she was driven before the wind for twenty-six hours, entirely unmanageable. Around midnight she went aground off Norbreck. Eight succeeded in struggling ashore to Bispham homes where they were cared for, but Captain James Quaint and three others were washed up opposite Rossall Hall, to be buried later at Bispham Church. Even the heavy iron steamships *Her Majesty* and *Royal Consort*, travelling from Ireland, took a buffeting and were several hours late. The Formby lightship was driven from its moorings, causing more accidents. Several vessels near Kingstown were wrecked as the gales on the Irish coast were violent indeed.

Underwriters were prejudiced against the new iron steamships even though they could sail faster, displaced less water suffered no damage from rot or rats and several watertight compartments could be made – this last of great importance for perishable cargoes. The fear was of so much iron acting on the ship's compass, but the *Economist* of 1845 reported iron steamships rapidly coming into use.

The destruction of the barque *Henry* off the Fylde coast in 1845 figured alongside the report of the smashing of the Portland Vase, one of the nation's treasures, but the description of the largest steamer in the world, the *Great Britain* took precedence. As she lay in Coburg Dock, Liverpool, in July, trips were organised to view her 180 staterooms and six masts. In the following month there began the trial of ten Portuguese and Spaniards charged with piracy on the high seas and the murder of an Englishman.

A useful chart covering the approaches to Morecambe Bay was issued on 8 April 1846 by permission of the Lords of the Admiralty. The man responsible, Henry Smith, had worked very hard to make the new port of Fleetwood a success, and his early death in a railway accident at Wolverton was a tragedy. In January a vessel was cast ashore near the mouth of the Ribble four miles from Blackpool, the property of Sir John Tobin, bound from Liverpool to an African port, laden with gunpowder and spirits. A Liverpool steam tug tried to pull her off but she had to be unloaded. Lloyds reported the losses in March of the barque *Ida* (550 tons) and the *John Mintura* taking government stores to Canada. The latter sailed on 4 January under Captain William Chamber. She was thrown on her beam ends in a severe gale from south-south-east and most of the passengers and crew rushed into the longboat, in all 45, but at about two cable lengths from the vessel she shipped a sea that capsized her and all in her perished. The few who remained on the wreck from Monday until Friday were taken off by the schooner *Three Sisters*. That year the Shipwrecked Mariners' Society reported that they were short of funds and made appeals for help. Liverpool Bay, over the centuries has seen innumerable shipwrecks and in the last hundred years, with the help of divers, most valuables have been salvaged, but a cargo of 13,000 silver dollars has never been traced. This was carried all the way from Valparaiso in the *Mary Scott*, a ship of 300 tons, together with other cargo worth £35,000.

After rounding Cape Horn and covering oceans, it may have been a relief on the night of 10 May for Captain Sadler to see the light of Point Lynas, but a cruel turn of luck set fate on a collision course. A large American ship, the *Brooklyn*, leaving Liverpool with emigrants hoping to start a new life in the New World, struck the *Mary Scott*'s starboard quarter with disastrous results to the smaller vessel. The *Brooklyn*'s bowsprit tore away her rigging, smashing the mainmast. Blocks and spars falling on the main deck badly hurt Captain Sadler and broke the carpenter's arm; other wreckage temporarily trapping the mate. Five feet of water rapidly filled the *Mary Scott*'s hold. It was apparent that she was a total wreck. Two days later a Manx fishing boat picked up seven survivors from the *Mary Scott*'s jolly boat who had bailed continuously for twenty-four hours to keep afloat. The long-boat, with the captain and crew, was never seen again. Such a valuable cargo attracted many hopefuls but, the point of collision in Liverpool Bay not being known, no amount of hunting brought evidence. Other wrecks were found from time to time and probed, but the silver from the *Mary Scott* is still awaiting retrieval.

Shortly after this episode there was another collision off the Magizines on 25 May in the Mersey between the Irish steamers *Sea Nymph* and *Rambler* with much loss of life.

An extraordinarily high tide off the Fylde coast in February 1847, the year that Queen Victoria visited Fleetwood, did great damage, Rossall Landmark was undermined and a farm nearby, Fenny, had its furniture washed out of doors, the residents fleeing for their lives. This farm was moved back four times and eventually abandoned as the force of the seas continually ate into the land, causing erosion at an astonishing rate. The barque *Hillsborough*, sailing from Lytham on 16 September, was wrecked on Ribble Banks with the loss of all hands. 'It was a cheerless evening, blowing hard,' wrote Queen Victoria in her diary as they arrived in the Fylde. The Independent Chapel, in the course of construction on the sandhills, was blown down and the Fleetwood Commissioners, who declared the weather 'too boisterous', said, 'No', to aquatic sports, replacing them with horse racing on the sands.

The burning of the *Ocean Monarch*, one of Train's Boston line of packet ships, occurred in the middle of the night, only two miles distant from home shores, its blaze being clearly seen from Blackpool Promenade. Filled with emigrants whose only choice was death by fire or water, she had sailed from Liverpool on 24 August 1848 with a passenger list as follows: 'Steerage 322: First and Second Cabin 32; Captain and crew 42'. Soon after the pilot and steam tug had left, a steward rushed on deck reporting to the captain that a passenger had lit a fire in one of the ventilators, which

Queen Victoria's visit to 'the newest port in her dominion', 1847. The *Royal Yacht* travelled from Scotland to Fleetwood in tempestuous seas that delayed the visit by two days. The Queen was pregnant at the time and Prince Albert commanded the captain 'to place the yacht in calmer waters'!
Captain William Swarbrick, pilot, guided the flotilla of yachts into Fleetwood Harbour and the Royal party spent the night on board. The train waits to take the Queen to London the next day. On the right can be seen the masts and funnel of the *Royal Yacht*.

had taken firm hold. In less than five minutes the whole after-part of the ship burst into flames. The passengers, in terrified confusion, crowded to the bowsprit to avoid the fire, many leaping overboard in despair, only to be drowned. Such was the hubbub that life-saving instructions went unheard. The captain, aided by the carpenter, flung over the side a top-gallant yard with rope attached, and as the flames were rapidly approaching he too leapt overboard. Too many people were clinging to the spar, so he swam to a floating board and within half an hour was picked up by Mr Thomas Littledale's yacht *Queen of the Ocean*, out on a pleasure trip with a party of friends from Liverpool.

Thirty-two lives were saved by this yacht. Meanwhile the Brazilian War Steamer *Alphonso*; the *Prince of Wales* steamer bound for Bangor; and the packet ship *New World* sent their boats. In minutes witnesses saw mizzen-mast and main-mast go overboard. As the fire made its way to the fore-part of the vessel, passengers and crew crowded further forward, clustered thickly, clinging to the jib-boom which, with its increasing load of human beings, inevitably dropped into the water amidst heart-rending screams. Mr J. Bragdon, mate of the *Ocean Monarch*, who was later commended for his bravery and humanity, recalled that the *Prince of Wales* could not approach, but she promptly sent her boats out; she also furnished more oars and more men. 'I endeavoured to get under the bows of the burning ship but utterly

Rossall Hall beside a rough sea, 1840.

The emigrant ship *Ocean Monarch*, soon after leaving Liverpool in August 1848, was lost in a catastrophe by fire at sea. Many jumped overboard to escape. Dead bodies were washed up along the Fylde at Blackpool, Bispham and Lytham. An entire Irish family was buried in Lytham churchyard. Ten years later, on 18 September 1858, the *Austria*, shown here, another emigrant ship (2,383 tones, Caird & Co.), carrying 538 passengers and crew, met a similar fate. The ship's surgeon was fumigating steerage quarters when a flaming bucket of tar was dropped. 471 persons were burned or drowned.

failed in persuading the passengers to come down. Only two could I save and put on board the Alphonso.'

Frederick Jerome, a sailor from the New World, climbed naked into the head of the *Ocean Monarch*, lowering fifteen passengers by line into the boats. Many had been drowned whilst stampeding from the heat, and by the time the last person was lowered by Jerome the whole of the upper deck was burnt out, fire bursting through the ship's sides down to the water's edge. The exiled Prince de Joinville, on board the *Alphonso* (which saved 139 persons), did a sketch of the horrific scene, which was later sold for a good sum and put towards the relief of the survivors, for which purpose £4,012 was raised. Liverpool rose to the tragic occasion with the greatest kindness as news of the disaster spread.

Yet another emigrant ship to perish this way was the *St George* which sailed from Liverpool on 24 December 1852, bound for New York with a miscellaneous cargo of iron, coal and oil besides 121 emigrants and a crew of twenty-five. All the passengers apart from four were Irish. To add to the terrors of fire, '... The weather was appalling. That night it blew a hurricane. In the course of thirteen years as a seaman I never experienced such weather'. Yet, such is the brotherhood of the sea, trip after trip was made by the lifeboat of the *Orlando* in an attempt to rescue the passengers who were too gripped by terror to jump and thus take the only chance they had of survival. Anyone who fell into the sea was immediately lost. Disgracefully, the captain of the *St George* deserted his ship in the early stages and the officers' behaviour appears to have been little better. 'There was not one left behind who knew how to manage the ship – the wheel was lashed'. Agents of the *St George* in Liverpool were Messrs Tapscott & Co., St George's Buildings.

When the going got tough it is evident that emigrants' lives were expendable. Conditions are known to have been appalling on board some of these ships, added to which this report from a surviving seaman of the *William and Mary*, an emigrant ship which sailed from Liverpool on 24 March 1853, speaks for itself:

> The Captain was the last to get into the longboat and even then he had to be urged very strongly before he consented to leave the vessel. When the passengers saw him go they knew there was no longer any hope. The poor creatures became frantic with despair. Six of the crew who still remained in the ship got ready the lifeboat into which several of the passengers jumped. I never saw anything in my life more fearful. One of the crew was compelled to keep off the passengers with a hatchet, otherwise the boat would undoubtedly have been swamped.

It was all in the day's work for frail barques to undertake hazardous ocean voyages. Vessels of 500 tons and under carried thousands of migrants to America and Australia, so casualties which befell the emigrants were heavy indeed. The wonder is that losses were not even more in ships made of wood, when steel wire rigging was unknown and the seas imperfectly charted. 3,760 ships entered Liverpool in 1848 and 131,000 emigrants sailed away to different parts of the world, which gives some idea of sea traffic from one port alone. The ship *Providence*, sailing to Africa, foundered in a severe gale in the Mersey Channel with the loss of thirty lives on 7 October 1870. The year before over 4,000 people had died of cholera in Liverpool and there were outbreaks all over the country. Perhaps some emigrants hoped to avoid the disease by taking a change of air. Lytham Lifeboat Fund was launched on 18 June 1851 with John Talbot Clifton heading the list of donors (£50). It is surprising that lifeboats were so scarce when danger constantly pronounced itself and there was no lack of bravery coming to the fore in men's endeavours to save their fellow-men. Fleetwood suffered a fearful hurricane in 1852 at the Christmas season 'when slates, hoardings, chimneys and people were whirled to the ground', yet did not get its first lifeboat until 1859. Moored in the Canshe Hole and deemed safe, the barque *Hope* capsized in this storm. Some seamen had carelessly left open the large square opening in her bows through which cargoes of timber were loaded. Into this yawning gap the seas came hurtling and the watchman had much ado to save himself before *Hope* settled on the river bed. She was an ill-fated ship who made voyages to Sydney, Calcutta, St Helena and Valparaiso. Built by James Lewtas, who came from Voss in Norway and lived at Stalmine Grange, the *Hope*, largest ship ever launched at Wardleys, was burned out on the high seas on 27 February 1862. For many years her log books and ship's bell were kept by the Lewtas family, but these items were stolen from a barn and the only relic remaining is a copper jug gracing a home on Whiteholme Estate, Norbreck.

The oceans added blow on blow for shipping in the mid-nineteenth century. The Collins steamer *Arctic* from Liverpool to New York was lost to a collision, only fifty-nine out of 381 people saved (27 September 1854). Another Collins steamship, the *Pacific*, also sailing from Liverpool to New York on 23 January 1816 was not heard of again, and that same year a gale raging for days drove many vessels from their moorings in the Mersey, stranding them upon the banks of the river and even battering together, with attendant damage, ships moored in the docks. On 6 February two steamers, the *Excelsior* and the *Mail*, collided off New Brighton; eight people were killed and six severely injured. The captain of the schooner *British Token* told his crew on 24 November 1870, 'You must prepare for Heaven or Hell for we are on those infernal Ribble Banks'. His cargo of oat meal swelled by the waves, burst open holds, but to the ever-hungry on shore it may have proved to be Lytham's 'oatmeal year'. The 1870s continued stormy. In October 1857, *Splendid* was wrecked off Bernard's Wharf; November, the *Norden*; December, *Samnauth* – both of Fleetwood. In December also the *Pilgrim* came to grief off the Isle of Man.

August 1859 found the *Sir Colin Campbell* stranded near the Landmark, but it was the *Royal Charter* with a cargo amounting to £273,000 from the goldfields of Australia and £48,000 in sovereigns as well as the fortunes of 400 passengers that attracted the whole nation's attention. The fastest ship on the Australian run, the Liverpool & Australian Steam Navigation Co.'s most famous clipper, accomplished the journey thirteen days faster than her nearest competitor. Captain Taylor left Melbourne for Liverpool on 26 August 1859, and after a round-the-world trip had the appalling luck to founder near home. She left Ireland slightly delayed as passengers wished to view the *Great Eastern* and moved into one of the worst storms ever experienced in England. The wind tore roofs from houses, killed 800 people and sank 133 ships. *Royal Charter*, heading for Liverpool ran into the teeth of the gale. As she reached Port Lynas, Captain Taylor sent up signals but no pilot could put out. Her anchors and engine useless against the fury of the sea, relentlessly this 2,719 ton passenger ship drifted, forced onto the rocks off Anglesey by 60ft waves on 26 October. The thirty-five passengers saved were on account of the bravery of Maltese seaman Joseph Rogers. Swimming ashore with a line around his body, he managed to rig up a bosun's chair but suddenly huge seas broke the clipper in two, drowning 459 people, including the captain and his officers. Within the next two months £320,000 worth of gold was recovered, but £30,000 was never accounted for, although cloudy speculation had it that local shore dwellers retrieved some and held their tongues. Certainly the wreck's fabulous quality is still discussed over pints of beer, like the wreck of the brigantine *Morning Star* in

Uncle Tom's cabin, Blackpool, where the brig *Portia* came ashore in 1850, the crew landing in the ship's boat.

1822 off Southport, laden with gold dust and ivory from Africa. Locals talked of gold being 'ladled out of pint pots', but in fact the cargo was all saved and taken to Lytham.

The wreck of the *Ocean Monarch* occupies a foremost place in maritime disasters and the narrative of a survivor from the *Caleb Grimshaw* emigrant ship, vividly re-lives the horror of another burning wreck. Sailing from Liverpool on 23 October 1849 with a general cargo and 427 passengers, fire was not discovered until 11 November, the ship being under full sail and travelling at 2 knots: 'In a few minutes all was confusion. The steerage passengers rushed up from their berths and came aft on the quarter-deck, lying and kneeling down, impeding the exertions of the crew and drowning the commands of the Captain with their cries... a considerable amount of water was got into the hold but still no abatement of smoke. The main hatch, which had been caulked over and pitched when leaving Liverpool, was opened and immediately thick volumes of smoke ascended. The hose was now diverted down this hatchway. The first mate, Mr Hoxie, volunteered to go down and try, if he could, to see the fire, but he had hardly been lowered when he called out immediately and said all was on fire below. Exertions at the pump were redoubled, and several of the passengers were set to work to assist the crew. Had the vessel had a gun on board, it ought to have been fired all night through but, strange to say, she was unprovided this way, nor had she any rockets or blue lights. Some ran to the captain's state room, beseeching him to save them, numbers crowded round the stern where the second mate was lowering ladies into the long-boat, others were seen at their prayers, husbands and wives embraced, mingling their tears. In the afternoon the captain was put on board the long-boat. 'O Captain dear, save us', cried the poor creatures on board on his leaving. Before he left, the crew made two more rafts. One of these was launched and thirty persons got on it, when, fearing it would be overcrowded, they cut themselves adrift. It is probable they all perished in a day or two as, although they had a barrel of beef and one of pork, they had very little water and no bread.

> As darkness set in, the wind increased to a gale and our situation in the Caleb Grimshaw was perilous. The vessel rolled in a fearful manner, dipping her studding sail booms in the water while at every roll the sea came in on the quarterdeck and sometimes even in the wheel house.
>
> At length morning broke, when we discovered to our great joy the Sarah five or six miles ahead… by dusk, she had taken off the burning vessel 133 persons including most of the women. On Tuesday 20th the sea was still running too high to remove the rest of the passengers but early the next morning the boat brought off five men who had been on board the wreck. They had a sad tale to tell. On Sunday night twenty had died, last night sixteen and four more this morning. Though most perished from thirst, it is probable some had poisoned themselves as they had broken into the Doctor's room and drunk laudanum and whatever other liquid they could find.

A Fylde diary entry for 1862 reads, 'I saw a beautiful vessel sail from Liverpool... crowded with emigrants going forth with hearts full of hope to settle in a foreign country. All round the pier and dock sides were standing groups of relatives and friends, some cheerful, some weeping...'

Liverpool was the chief port of emigration and if a disaster reduced demand, the falling off did not last long. The tide of emigration and the rush to the Australian and Californian goldfields was handled by such leading Merseyside firms as James Baines & Co., who had the Black Ball Line, Messrs Pilkington & Wilson, owners of the Liverpool White Star Line, James Beazley, Henry Fox, Miller & Thompson of the Golden Line and Fernie Brothers of the Red Cross Line. On 22 April 1858 the *James Baines*, a cloud of canvas in her heyday, was destroyed by fire, lying in Huskisson Dock where she had just arrived with a cargo. Two Cunarders had to be quickly moved out of danger and the burning masts, in failing, set two sheds alight. The ship was so badly burnt that the lower part or her hull could only be used afterwards as a floating landing stage. Ship and cargo were worth £170,000.

Anecdotes from such eye-witnessed drama pass down through families, whole communities and perhaps even across continents, living on into the present day. At Christmas 1981, from Recklinghausen, West Germany, came enquiries concerning the brig *Cornelia*, built in Papenburg, North Germany, which foundered off Peel on Man Flats on 21 December 1859. Doctor Hans Albe wrote:

> When my great-great-grandpa came from the shipbuilding yard in cold and stormy weather he found his mother Catharina sitting at open fire saying to him in Dialekt, 'Berend you hefft onse Willmeen Doadcnkist baut' (Berend you have built acoffin for our Willm!). Asking her why she should say this, she told him she had seen the coast of Britain with the wrecked ship. Some days later a letter came from Britain with the news.

The newspaper report following this event reads as follows:

> Intelligence has been received at Fleetwood of the total loss of five vcssels off the coast of Lancashire in a squall on Tuesday night. The first is the schooner Pilgrim of Douglas, Isle of

Veering down on a wreck.

> Man – the vessel foundered off the coast of Blackpool but the master and men succeeded in landing at Baycliffe in an open boat. It is expected that some part of the vessel and cargo may be saved as the topgallant and topsails can be seen above the low watermark. The Master of this vessel reports that he saw a schooner in a sinking state not far from where his vessel went down. A brig laden with Indian corn also foundered about six miles south of Walney light. The fourth is a schooner bound from Liverpool to Limerick which went down not far distant from where the brig laundered. The crew of the schooner look refuge on Fouly Island much exhausted, having suffered severely from the frost. The schooner has disappeared but the brig is visible six miles S.S.E. of the Walney light. The fifth wreck is that of a schooner which stranded at the North End of Walney Island, but coastguards have saved the crew and part of the cargo. We have not been able to arrive at the names or four of these ill-fated vessels.
> (*Fleetwood Chronicle*, 23 December 1859)

It is obvious that the *Cornelia* went down in good company.

4

REAP THE WHIRLWIND

The number of calls for help made on one seaside town alone is proved by 'returns of the Services of the Lifeboat at Fleetwood', which reports on launchings in the 1860s. Because of increased commercial traffic, shipwrecks began to read like an on-going list. As the Industrial Revolution gathered momentum, more and more steamships were driven ever faster whilst the tall sailing ships still plied the sea lanes.

No sooner had January 1860 been ushered in with the usual attendant gales and high seas than twenty-two riggers were drowned opposite Brunswick Dock, Liverpool, by the swamping of their boat as it returned from work aboard the emigrant ship *Trianon*. A famous captain, linked with Liverpool, William Harrison of the *Great Eastern* steamship, was mourned in the same month for the same reason. His impressive funeral was attended by officers and men of the Cunard Line of Packets and by Liverpool merchants.

With the arrival of the first unnamed lifeboat at Fleetwood, records speak for themselves. The crew showed that skill gained in their daily calling as fishermen was of great advantage in rescue work. They were soon very busy building up the most distinguished record of all lifeboatmen round the Fylde coast, vigorously living up to the traditions of the Royal National Lifeboat Institution, which was founded in 1824 'for the preservation of life from shipwreck'. The following are typical entries from the Record of Launchings:

22 Jan. 1860 Ann Mitchell, James Chalmers Master-cargo of oats to Liverpool W.S.W. Gale Force 10 wrecked on Barnett Wharf; one life saved, 3 lost due to stress of weather, loss of compass and sails. Total wreck. Lifeboat launched 6 p.m. Return to shore 2.40 a.m. on 23 January.

23 Jan. 1860 Schooner Jane Roper. Master, William Harris – sailing from Ardrossan with pig iron. W.S.W. strong gale. Wrecked on Shell Wharf and sunk – all crew saved. Anchor, cable and boathook lost from lifeboat. Oar found at Clevelass.

Feb. 19, 1860 Schooner Catherine of Norway sailing from Newry to Fleetwood with timber. W.N.W. gale stranded on Barnett's Wharf, 4 lives saved. '20 oct. 1860 The Barque Vennont of Halifax. 528 tons and crew of l5. Carrying timber. Parted from her anchors and drove on Barnett Wharf, 3 miles off Fleetwood. Launched lifeboat 10 a.m. Taken in tow by steam tug Adjutant and towed to windward at 10.30 a.m. reached the wreck and rescued the crew and pilot.

> 2 Nov. 1861 Britannica, a sloop carrying coal was discovered on shore on the North Wharf, close to the perch with crew in the rigging. Lifeboat was launched and manned and made an attempt to reach the wreck but unable to do so and had to remain until the tug got up steam. Owing to the tide blowing (N.N.E. gale) and the sloop's scamsail being partially set, heavy seas sank her and the crew disappeared. When the lifeboat reached the wreck she remained some time but saw nothing of the crew. Paid each man 10/- and two 1/- for assisting to house the boat. The crew could have been saved had the lifeboat been double-banked. In addition to want of power, crew had not room to work the oars properly.

The laconic reference to the schooner *Jane Raper*, January 1860, was an incident in one of the most destructive storms which ever caused loss of life and chaos. The barque *Tyne*, bound for Glasson Dock with corn for Mr Rawsthorn, a merchant, had been riding at anchor in the Lune for almost a week, awaiting the spring tides, but under the skilful management of John Grimshaw, pilot, she ran for Fleetwood and came safely alongside the pier head. A barque, seen 'dodging' near North Wharf, caused anxiety as she obviously did not know the harbour approaches. Schooner Thomas Whitworth arrived in the Wyre with several of her sails blown away, the tattered remnants streaming like pennants from the yard arms and bowsprit, her bulwarks showing evidence of having encountered severe seas. The flat *Arthur*, laden with coals for Greenodd, sank in the bight of the Channel off the coastguard station. During the afternoon the *Telulah* of Savannah, laden with cotton, anchored westward off the Screw Pile lighthouse. As evening came on, three other vessels were seen bearing down for Morecambe Bay – the barque *Victoria* from Liverpool to Mobile, the schooner *Anna Dixon* from Sligo for Liverpool with oats, and the schooner *Jane*

On 10 February 1860 the scene was not so calm. Five vessels were damaged in a gale in Fleetwood Harbour, although moored at the quay with strong hawsers. Cotton-laden, the *Refuge* snapped her stern moorings and set off a chain reaction due to the tremendous rush of water. The barge *Redlickeit*, full of coal and set for Rio de Janeiro, filled with water. Collision upon collision followed until every vessel as far as the bend of the quay parted from its moorings. An anchor struck *Mary Rosanna*, laden with pig iron, and she drifted towards the *Redlickeit*. The scene was one of total confusion and the damage tolled £3,000.

Roper of Barrow from Newport for Morecambe. The *Victoria* rode out the gale in safety but the schooners exhibited signals of distress. The *Anna Dixon* foundered upon Bernard's Wharf and was utterly lost. The *Jane Roper* sank off Shell Wharf, a bank south-west of Rossall Landmark. Only the upper ponions of her masts and rigging remained above water, and to these the crew of six clung for safety all night.

Their perilous position was seen early in the morning by the tug *Adjutant*, who towed the lifeboat out to rescue them. The *Telulah*, in running with the tide, grounded on the Knott. The barque near North Wharf, which proved to be the *Charles Brunel* from Singapore for Liverpool with general cargo, was reported to be making much water and in danger of sinking. Badly mutilated and entangled in the ship's rigging, the body of one man was later recovered from the *Anna Dixon* which broke up, portions of the rigging and cables being the only salvage, whilst the cargo from the *Charles Brunel* was wasted.

Nine days later a crew of six were saved from the brig *Sister Anne*, carrying iron ore from Whitehaven to Swansea. Meanwhile the Reverend Thornber was trying to get a lifeboat for Blackpool, appealing for funds in 1862 (£30 from Mr John Pickup, £100 from Sir Bernard Heywood, £250 from Mrs Hopkins). On 14 July 1864 the *Robert William* was launched with blue-eyed Bob Bickerstaffe as coxswain and a crew of fourteen, its first turn-out to the brig *Michael*. John Bickerstaffe, later Mayor and chairman of the Blackpool Tower Co., was also a member of that crew.

A phenomenally low tide at the ebb in 1860 revealed the Pennystone high and dry, and the skeer behind 'Th 'owd woman's hood' lain bare for the first time in the memory of the oldest Blackpool inhabitant. Folk tales of church bells ringing from the submerged ancient villages of Amounderness, the sound of the carousing from ghostly hostelries muffled by the crash of waves were revived, and would-be archaeologists set off with shovels to explore, taking advantage of the rare tides' ebb.

By contrast, in 1862, an extraordinary rise in the tides occurred. It was the year of the *Great Eastern*'s first entry into the Mersey (4 June) after making the passage from New York with a large cargo and 212 passengers in nine days and eleven hours. Even with six masts, five funnels and a crew of 397, she suffered from gales before the year was out. With her steering apparatus damaged, for two days and nights she was exposed to heavy seas which played havoc with interior fittings. Early 1863 had storm and flood raging for twenty-four hours. The wall of the Mount at Fleetwood, brought to light by November gales after having long been buried in sand, was washed down on 20 January 1863; the White Houses (site of the present Mount Hotel) likewise. As one resident put it, 'The sea gave us notice to quit'.

The lifeboat house was destroyed and only with great difficulty was the boat retrieved. A wooden battery of two 32-pounder guns at the foot of the Mount, belonging to the coastguards, became so undermined it had to be removed. Sea defences between the Landmark and Cleveleys were swept away; streets flooded and the inn keeper and

Right: A wreck off Formby – the stormy 1860s.

Below: The *Great Eastern* at Liverpool in the seedy latter days of her career. Hailed as the wonder and failure of her age, she was built by John Scott Russell and Co. for the Eastern Steam Navigation Co., Scott Russell and Isambard Kingdom Brunel being the brains behind her design. The huge ship ruined the company.

his family at Strawberry Gardens Hotel were rescued by boat. At Lytham the barque *Reuben* got into difficulty. The lifeboat, hauled by eight horses, could not be launched until they reached five miles further down the coast where conditions were not as bad. Incidentally, Lytham had its first boat, *Eleanor Cecily*, in 1851, its station established by the Shipwrecked Fishermen and Mariners' Royal Benevolent Society, but there was a boat in 1844, making Lytham the oldest lifeboat station on the Flyde coast. With a crew of fourteen wearing harnesses and corkjackets, this boat was propelled by 14ft-long ash oars and sails. Launchings took place from the old boathouse by the windmill, often with the whole town helping. Horses and men dragged the boat into the sea whilst the coxswain, watching for a good sized wave, would signal for all helpers to 'haul on the launching falls.'

The second lifeboat at Fleetwood (the timber of the first was sold for £165 and the replacement building erected for £162) was built inland of brick, facing tall Pharos Lighthouse, but in later years, as launching was not easy several hundred yards from the shore, the lifeboat house was again sited on the beach, although the persistent problem of blowing sands clogging the launching slope made it necessary to move the building bodily to a better position, but even that did not solve matters. Sir Peter Hesketh Fleetwood wrote once again to brother Charles on 21 February 1863, 'You will have heard how heavy the damage at Rossall was this Autumn – many thousands of pounds to me.' 15 March 1863, 'I have suffered greatly at Rossall Sea Wall, which required large supplies of cash to repair – last year was terribly rough but the mode of groynes I have adopted will, I think, prevent the necessity of walls. What an awful night of wind it was – may the Sea Defences keep right.' It was in the Great Storm of January 1863 that Lytham's old stone light house, built on a gravel stanner and having withstood many years, suddenly crumbled and fell, according to local gossip coinciding exactly with the fall of the mast of the *Reuben* 'on a terrible high tide'.

On 20 October 1862 a vessel, the *Quasi Rosa*, struck Trunk Hill Bank and capsized after two masts went overboard. In such heavy seas the crew had no chance. Three days later a parcel of letters was washed up at Ainsdale, the manifest of the Italian *Quasi Rosa*, en voyage from Ardrossan to Genoa with a crew of thirteen. She was completely fragmented by the seas, which strewed wreckage from Ainsdale to Marshside and battered the *Ann E. Hooper*, a barque bringing flour, tallow and wheat from Baltimore to Liverpool. Two masts were cut away during the gale in a bid to lighten the 1,144-ton American cargo

Wooden lifeboat house, Fleetwood.

Another unnamed wreck thought to have been battered in an 1860s' storm, coming ashore at Cleveleys where the *Ann Paley*, Liverpool to Lisbon bound, was wrecked. She fired distress guns but three of her crew were swept overbaord, chests of tea littered the shore and at Lytham, on the same night, fifteen vessels were damaged.

At Glasson, a wet dock 500ft long and 200ft wide was constructed in 1783 on the east bank of the river, necessary for mooring vessels like the schooner *Mary Barrow*, because of silting at the port of Lancaster about five miles away. The crew of seventeen, shipwrecked from the *Pudyona*, were landed here in 1862.

vessel. As a Liverpool tug battled to get her going, such a west-north-west hurricane built up that she was stationary for an hour. Two seamen were washed off the deck of the barque and, both vessels being in danger, the low rope had to part. *Ann E. Hooper* drifted onto the Horsebank. She could be seen four miles north of Southport Pier, and the new lifeboat *Jessie Knowles* set off at 7 a.m. with William Rockcliffe (cox), Ben Ball, Geoff Ball, J. Ball, William Rigby, Peter Bolton, Peter Jackson, William Robison, Geoff Rockcliffe, Thomas Such, and John and Thomas Wright. Lytham lifeboatmen arrived at the wreck first as they were towed all the way. They took off twelve men and the Southport boat rescued Captain Hooper and three seamen. Before the arrival of the lifeboats, two of the barque's crew drowned in a desperate attempt to launch one of the vessel's own lifeboats. Not to be outdone, the old lifeboat *Rescue* and three Meols fishermen also went out to the wreck and salvaged the crew's belongings when the tide went down. As the barque broke up it was swept against the pier, carrying away one of its supports. 1,500 casks of flour, tallow and lard were washed ashore and taken to Rockcliffe's Yard in Eastbank Street. Residents filched the tobacco but found the bacon uneatable, and clocks, also part of the cargo, were discovered years later hidden in thatched roofs. The good oak from the decking was made into various articles including a coffin and a cradle, such symbolism inspiring a poem from lifeboatman and ship's chandler William Bolton.

Much mischief was done by the gales of 1862 and 1863. On 27 October 1862 the barque *Pudyona*, owned by Mr John Stamp Burrell of Lancaster, was being aided by the steam tug *Teazer* when her tow rope parted when they were halfway to Glasson, one mile east of Danger Patch. The ship struck with such force that the masts went overboard, carrying all her rigging with them, leaving the vessel at the mercy of the sea. The crew clung on, trying not to be washed off. The *Teazer* could not help, but Captain William Swarbrick of Fleetwood hailed from his steam tug *Wyre* asking if the crew had been saved. Hearing that they had not, Swarbrick was determined to try. Masts and rigging made it impossible to approach on the lee side whilst the sea was heating up against her starboard side, which was to windward. To approach here was a dangerous task. However, the tug was run alongside her starboard quarter and the *Pudyona*'s crew, who had stationed themselves on that side of the vessel, leapt aboard the *Wyre*. When Captain Swarbrick arrived at the wreck the port side was out and cargo could be seen through her stern. The ill-fated *Pudyona* was driven relentlessly over the bank into the swashway and went down in deep water. Next the *Wyre* proceeded to assist the brig *Marys* of Glasson Dock, bound for Miramichi with timber. With both her anchors down and dragging, she was making signals for help, so the tug took her in tow, arriving at Glasson Dock at 3 p.m., the crew were dropped off and the *Wyre* returned to Fleetwood.

Captain Connell's ship, the *Content*, and the schooner Warree, under Captain Jennings, put into Morecambe with their sails blown away. 280 logs of timber were washed ashore

Eleanor Cecily.

Above: Glasson Dock, near Lancaster.

Left: The carved figurehead of the *Circasian*, moored at Liverpool in 1868 alongside *Abyssinia*, weathered storms aplenty. In the days of sailing ships the figurehead was important as it was believed it affected the fortunes of the ship. Great woodcarvers like Grining Gibbons designed for the man o' wars of the seventeenth century.

with 360 pins of lathwood, 210 spokes and 375 deals – all from the *Pudyona.* 'The bay is completely full of timber and wreck,' reported the newspapers, with the added item that the Screw Pile Lighthouse on Clark's Wharf, Morecambe Bay, was so badly damaged by the gales 'as to render uncertain the light being constantly visible.'

Captain Rawsthorne, Harbourmaster, called attention to this dauntless bravery in an address to the Shipwrecked Fishermen and Mariners' Society. In 1863, 'for the rescue of a whole ship's company', silver medals and vellum scrolls were presented to Captain William Swarbrick and pilots Gerrard, Hornby and Hesketh. The *Pudyona*, built in Nova Scotia in 1851, 134ft long, was registered at Lancaster under the official number 17790.

In January 1863 rescue of a barque on Salthouse Bank, Lytham, necessitated transporting the lifeboat on her carriage for five miles, a long, hard pull by eight horses. Forty-four lives had been saved in three months at Lytham by this date. The Ribble overflowed its banks; damage was reported all down the coast and inland. In Blackpool there were fears for the safety of the pier 'now in course of erection'. Tremendous

Liggard Brook and the site of the Lytham Shipbuilding & Engineering Co. Ltd. The yacht *Nancy*, belonging to the Clifton family, was moored in Nancy's Bay.

seas sent planks flying and wind pressure at Liverpool Observatory was 43lb to the square foot at the height of the gale, which astonished even the oldest inhabitants. All seaports had been telegraphed by Admiral Fitzroy warning that a fierce gale was expected, thus some disasters to shipping were avoided. The River Mersey had 'never looked so grandly picturesque', the West Quays of George's and Brunswick Docks being flooded. Captain Somer's ship, the *J.H. Elliot*, bound for New York, and Messrs Battersby & Co.'s ship *Admiral*, bound for Bombay, both turned back but touched Burbo Bank. The first-mentioned burnt out as her cargo of phosphorus ignited; the second sank to her decks in sand, but all twenty-nine of her crew were saved.

The *Constantine*, a full-rigged ship of 2,000 tons burthen, from New York with a cargo of Indian corn and lard and fourteen passengers, was soon in difficulty. The *Wyre* of Fleetwood and the *Talbot* of Liverpool towed her to Liverpool. Off Blackpool the vessel had her masts cut away to prevent her driving on shore. Anchors were let go and she struck bottom twice, but they held her. If she had gone ashore there would have been little hope for crew and ship, Two Blackpool coastguards, W. Mitch and W. Pierce, bravely went into the surf with ropes tied round them when the ship's boat capsized, and assisted in rescuing the crew. *Princess Marie* was wrecked on Pilling Sands. A hole was cut in her bottom and most of her damaged cargo saved, but as she lay keel upwards, attempts to tow her failed and the authorities reported, 'nothing can be done until the Spring tides'.

The *Nancy*, on her way from Dumfries in the same gale, parted her anchors at Barrow and went ashore on Railway Bank, south-east of the town, but it was possible the next day to take off all her timber. The schooner *Ceres* of Arbroath struck heavily on Salthouse Bank off Lytham. The lifeboat was launched and managed to get the schooner (whose pumps were kept going all the time) off on the next tide. Praise abounded for the Lytham lifeboat under John Edmondson for first-class order and instantaneous action.

Amongst Lancaster registered vessels, the *Dora*, a sailing vessel built at Ulverston in 1836, 59ft long, was reported 'lost off Holyhead on 2 May 1862, certificate of registry lost with vessel'. She was a wooden, carvel-built schooner with two masts. The *Frederick and Betsey*, a wooden carvel-built sailing vessel with dandy rigging and a round stern, was lost under mysterious circumstances. The Register of Ships records her as 55ft-long and weighing 43 tons, numbered 1666, 'lost about the year 1864 near to Liverpool'.

Schooners and cargo boats like the *Jessie Stewart* and *Mary Rosanna*, whose freight books are still in existence, did mainly coastal work, carrying coal and pig-iron to Ardrossan. Their seaworthiness having been neglected could soon put them in jeopardy. Boys of ten might be part of the crew, earning 2/- a week. Hauling 181 tons of iron at 4/- a ton, the owner's share equalled the captain's for a trip (£12-18-5¼). Some boys, smitten with sea fever, ran away from home at ten, twelve or fourteen years of age, drawn by questing spirit, expressed in the glamour of windjammers. One of these, Captain John Peattie of St Annes, sailed round the world thirty times, having command of fourteen vessels. In 1863 he sailed to Melbourne in an iron ship at a time when only the *Great Britain*, the *Simla* and the *London* were sailing to the Colonies. He experienced wreck, fire and 'a ship that sat on her anchor and sank', but he always went back.

Unlike the dirty and sometimes dangerous cargo boats, the larger vessels were well organised with careful lists of stores made and full preparation for long voyages. The condition of all the sails was recorded: 'foresail, topsail, main Royal, moonsail, crossjack, main topsail, main topgallant, mizzen, sky sail mizzen, Royal main Spencer' – marked 'good' or 'half good'. The stores on board the *Cicero* in July 1867 included awnings, bolts of canvas for repair and making of new sails, clewliney, buntliney, extra rope, pitch, Stockholm tar, skyrockets, nails, screws, cabin lamps, boards, gunpowder, blocks and deck stanchions. It is interesting to note that the drinks included 60 gallons of lime juice. (High in vitamin C content, lime juice was found to prevent the fatal disease (amongst sailors) of scurvy.) Firkins of butter, bladders of lard, molasses, 'cooly' rice, flour, ham, currants, potatoes – a huge supply of food was taken on board, for a voyage

Small shrimpers and fishing boats worked from Norbreck, near Blackpool.

might last ten weeks or more. In heavy seas, preparation of hot food became impossible and the crew could be wet and shivering for days. It helped to sing sea shanties like '*Old Stormy's dead and gone to rest*'. Sailors used to say that a good shanty was worth ten men on a rope, but working a sailing ship was demanding of superhuman effort, the ship's master shouldering colossal responsibility. On this particular voyage out of Fleetwood Captain Monk of the *Cicero* was given friendly advice on Bills of Lading: '... before signing read carefully. A Captain should never sign a bill of lading unless it is properly stamped – no merchant can compel him to do so; by doing so he is under a penalty of £50.' As a final piece of advice the captain was cautioned never to lose his temper. One wonders what breed of men were these who could shoulder hardship, responsibility, have the care of ship and crew always at heart, impose unquestioning discipline and be commanding of respect. Such salt of the sea was Captain William Swarbrick... 'hands like cabbage leaves he could fell a man at one blow but was as gentle as a lamb with his wife'. On trial in the 1860s was a sea captain who had 'gone at his crew with a cutlass', causing one poor fellow, the mate, to jump overboard and drown.

The Lancaster registered sailing ship *Buccleuch*, built in 1863, 108ft-long, 207 tons, on arrival in Rio de Janeiro, reported to the British Consulate who duly informed the Customs House at Lancaster: 'On the arrival of the Buccleuch at this port the Master reported that the register of his vessel had been entirely destroyed by rats during the voyage from the United States to this port ... such I believe to have been the case'.

The 1860s continued stormy, fifty-three lives being saved by the Fleetwood boat alone. In July 1862, five from the sloop *William*, sailing from Liverpool in October

1863, four from the schooner *Northern Light*, en route from Preston in October 1864, five saved – Brigantine *Highland Mary* from Troon. In January 1865, the *Lelia*, a cutter-rigged paddle steamer on her first voyage to Nassau from Liverpool with 700 tons of coal, was lost off the North West Light Ship, her crew of eighteen drowned with their captain. Whilst in attendance, No.1 lifeboat capsized, drowning seven of her crew. Captain William Swarbrick, in a different operation, once more towed the Fleetwood lifeboat out on 7 December 1866 to the dismasted barque *Inga*. A beautiful oil painting inscribed with the story of the rescue was done to commemorate this dramatic event, showing lifeboat and steam tug *Wyre* battling with mountainous waves. Thirteen lives were saved from the barque *Inga* travelling from Kragero. On 19 November 1867 the Greek steamer *Boubulina* exploded in the Mersey with the loss of nineteen lives.

Edwin Waugh, the Lancashire writer, wrote in 1869 of Norbreck, 'Everything smacks of the sea. On the grassy border of the road about the middle of the hamlet there is generally a pile of wreck waiting the periodical sale which takes place all along the coast. I have sometimes looked at this pile and thought to this or that spar some seaman might have clung desperately among the hungry waters until he sank'. At the Green, Southport, by William Rockcliffe's cottage in Eastbank Street, was stored wreckages of all kinds, guarded by a seagull, a terrifying bird who would allow no one near its territory. Captain Rockcliffe, receiver of wrecks and coxswain until his death in 1873, had an amazing record. He saved 367 lives in the *Rescue*, the first Southport boat, he brought ashore 212. In the *Jessie Knowles*, the first official lifeboat, seventy-one, and in

Market Street, Ulverston.

other boats eighty-four, on top of which he assisted in and piloted to safety seventeen vessels. Training a guard seagull would surely not be beyond him.

Although Southport had set up a Marine Fund in 1817 'to reward the inhabitants of this parish who saved lives and property in cases of shipwreck', the boat produced was totally unfit for rescue work and served instead as a pleasure craft. The year 1860 was a landmark in Southport 's history when Captain Ward of the RNLI offered to provide a 30ft lifeboat with transporting carriage if a new boathouse and upkeep were assured. This was agreed to and the lifeboat was launched on 9 September 1861 (*Jessie Knowles*), in the midst of a gale and with high seas in evidence to prove the necessity .

Meanwhile, Lancaster registered ships had also been affected. On 20 May 1866 *Annie Fisher*, a two-masted brig carvel built of wood, with a female figurehead, owned by James Fisher of Barrow, was reported thus: 'vessel abandoned at sea in a sinking state'.

The *Lucretia*, official number 54542, a sailing ship of 5½ tons, 261ft long, built at Barrow, was lost on Duddon Banks on 1 September 1866. *Baker*, a sailing vessel built at Ulverston in 1838, 59ft long and also registered at Lancaster, was wrecked off Piel Island in November 1867, closely followed by *Fanny Slater*, a sailing ship 87ft long, on 1 December. Carrying £650 worth of pig-iron from Fleetwood, she became a complete wreck near the Isle of Man, and the letter from the Receiver of Wrecks, Barrow in Furness, stated, 'the crew are all presumed to be lost'.

Elephant, official number 1508, a sailing ship, 60ft long, carvel-built in 1831 and owned by Robert Woodburn of Ulverston, was the subject of another letter from Barrow – 'the Certificate of Registry of the *Elephant* of Lancaster was lost with the vessel on the morning of the 19 October 1869 on Taylor's Bank outside the entrance of the River Mersey between Formby and the Crosby Lightships'.

Sailors and landlubbers long remembered the 1860s for extreme weather. In the great snowstorm of 12 January 1866 when the poles and wires of the telegraph between Liverpool and London broke for about sixty miles under the weight of snow and ice, all communication was suspended. Ice 7in thick was reported in March of that year, whilst May, with storm, sleet, snow and floods, killed hundreds of swallows. Indeed it was calculated that three ships a day were being lost round the British Isles.

5

The Stormalong Seventies

Wyre Light was 'a structure designed to save many a barque that would otherwise drive unbeaconed onto the sands of Morecambe Bay'. It suffered damage in 1870 when the Preston schooner *Elizabeth Jane* was driven by the tide, striking the Screw Pile lighthouse so that its upper structure fell upon the deck of the schooner and almost sank the latter with the additional weight. A tug towed schooner and strange cargo to port. Only one was injured and the top of the lighthouse was for a long time used by the coal gang as shelter. The tug *Jabez Bunting* was moored as a lightship but incidentally a new Wyre Light was provided as lightships had a bad habit of breaking loose in rough seas and causing havoc by misleading shipping. In the same year the steam tug *Brother Jonathan* sank off Prince's Pier, Liverpool, on 25 March. She was raised on 14 August. Sarah Louise Moore and W.C. Bennett were but two poets who in 1873 wrote of wrecks and lifeboat rescues ('Hurrah, to the wreck she goes'). But many disasters occurred with no witnesses.

Two Morecambe fishermen, John Edmondson and Adam Raby, were drowned from the fishing smack *Leader* on 29 May 1876 in unknown circumstances. Edmondson left a wife and eight children and came from a particularly unlucky family, six members of which had been killed. three from drowning. The Wreck Register presented by the Board of Trade to Parliament revealed numerous shipwrecks on all coasts during 1876-7, amounting to 4,164, exceeding the previous year's total by 407. 511 of these were total losses. Wrecks from 1857-76 had averaged 1,948 per year and represented millions of pounds lost, but the Wreck Abstract for the west coast did reveal 4,795 lives saved under *Shipping Intelligence* for 12 October 1877. A list of Fleetwood vessels at other ports totalled ninety-one. This was, of course, the month that the 1,000ft Wyre Dock was opened with much ceremony, an undertaking that had cost £400,000 and where 18,000 tons of grain alone could he stored.

Soon after the opening of New Promenade at Blackpool in 1870, the *Sprightly* of Preston, bound for Barrow with stone, got into difficulties in a south-westerly gale in the Lytham Channel. The crew of two let go the anchor and hoisted a flag of distress. They were rescued by the Robert William, William Parr being coxswain. From the timber of the wreck two huts were built on Chapel Street. On 25 July of the same year the fishing boat *Active* had to be helped by the lifeboat on the spot where the rich *Crusader* had gone down thirty-one years before.

In 1871 the Southport Lifeboat had been hauled on its carriage to Formby to rescue the 850-ton Liverpool barque *Times*, struck on Formby Point. The horses which pulled the lifeboat were often scared of the waves and would not face them, so a good launching position was difficult to achieve. In 1872 the *Nazarene* of 172 tons was driven onto Burbo Bank. New Brighton, Liverpool, and Formby lifeboats had searched unsuccessfully for this ship which had left the Mersey six days previously. Captain Rockcliffe was not prepared to risk crew and boat. The *Nazarene* became a total loss and her crew of sixteen men were all drowned.

Fleetwood lifeboat, *Child of Hale*.

In 1838 Fleetwood pilot boat No.2 was used by the Government in Morecambe Bay, for surveying the River Wyre. Twelve months later it was used as a fishing smack, but sank at the end of the stone pier in rough weather.

The *Wennington* at Lancaster, Shipowners' Quay 1865, the first iron clipper to be built at Lancaster. She was lost in unknown circumstances at sea in 1878.

As for Liverpool's losses, one heart-rending affair was the wreck of the sloop *Nelly*, under Captain Watson on 16 April 1870, which foundered in a gale. The captain's wife and four children went down with the vessel, and the fifth died in his father's arms. In the small boat which was picked up the next day, Captain Watson, utterly exhausted and distraught, was the only survivor.

The steamship *City of Boston*, belonging to Messrs Inman & Co., left for Liverpool from New York in January 1870, but no tidings of the steamer were to be had. A large vessel with many passengers and a crew of eighty-four, it was eventually accepted that she was lost in the hurricane of 29 January, reported by sailors to be one of the most terrible in recollection.

Of Lancaster vessels in the '70s, the *Chapultepec*, built in 1854, another sailing vessel owned by John Stamp Burrell, was so badly damaged by storms that on 14 November 1871 a letter from the Customs House at Liverpool reported, 'wreck of Chapultepec is now in course of being broken up'. The carvel-built sailing ship *Rajah Gopaul*, 156ft long, official number 1748, 811 tons, a three-master with a square stem built at Quebec in 1850, was wrecked on 4 September 1870.

The *Chieftain*, also Lancaster registered, was 'abandoned, waterlogged' bound from Miramichi to Glasson Dock on 3 December 1872 – yet another of Burrell's who delivered up the Certificate of Registry on 12 December 1872. But the pride and joy of Lancaster had been *Wennington*, an iron sailing ship of clench build, with three masts, square-rigged, round-sterned, 189ft long and 882 tons. Her owner was William A.F. Saunders of Wennington Hall. Most unusually she had a male bust for a figure-head. 'Vessel lost in the year 1878, date unknown', is the terse report in the Register of Ships. Built in Lancaster in 1865, she was launched in a carnival atmosphere, the first ship to be built by the Lune Shipbuilding Co. of Lancaster, which was formed in 1864. They built five sailing vessels between 1865 and 1869 and lost £13,000, so the company had to be wound up in 1870. Their bright hopes of rivalling Barrow and Liverpool dissolved like the cargo of sugar which the *Wennington* was carrying when she was lost at sea.

On Saturday 1 March 1873 the SS *Torch*, belonging to Dublin & Liverpool Screw S.S. Company, and the ship *Chicabuco* of Liverpool, homeward bound from San Francisco and loaded with grain, violently collided during a blinding snowstorm. The latter ship was so badly damaged from deck to water's edge that it sank in three minutes, drowning twenty-four out of twenty-seven. The three survivors swam clear and clung to floating wreckage until picked up by the steam tug *Guiding Star*. SS *Rover* had to tug back to port the badly damaged steamer *Torch*.

A telegram from New York the following month brought news of a disaster unparalled in maritime records. 'On Change' (in the Liverpool Exchange), in the Assize Courts, the Town Council, on every corner of every Liverpool street the sensational news of the sinking of *Atlantic*, a splendid White Star steamer, claiming 700 lives within fifteen minutes, was spoken of in hushed tones. Posted in the Exchange News Room, the information fell like a thunderbolt on the populace. The offices of Messrs Ismay, Imrie & Co. were besieged by anxious relatives. Mr C.L. Brady, the third officer, who had escaped, telegraphed that the magnificent vessel, built by Harland & Wolff of Belfast, 437ft long and 3,707 tons register, had been making her nineteenth voyage from Liverpool to New York in March under the command of Captain J.A. Williams. Gales reduced her speed and coal supplies became low, so it was considered necessary to put into Halifax. In this operation the *Atlantic* struck Mars Island and water poured in immediately. Companion-ways were blocked with the rush of passengers 'and as in all cases of shipwreck men became dazed, venturing on the first chance that presented itself of getting out of the vessel without a thought of consequences'. All six lifeboats succumbed immediately to the ice-cold hate and fury of the waves. On all sides people were falling from the ship's rigging'. Several, numbed with the cold and completely exhausted, lay down and died. Some foamed at the mouth like maniacs. At the Board of Trade enquiry the court censured Captain Williams but, considering the efforts he had made to save lives, his licence was not suspended but revoked for two years.

The following year news came of the sinking of a fine new ship built by Messr T. Royden of Liverpool, which had left with general cargo and eighty-nine emigrants. The vessel, chartered by the White Star Co., was totally wrecked, only nine people escaping death.

Nineteenth-century Certificates of Discharge show that Fleetwood boy David Singleton, one of three generations involved in navigation by sail, was serving on board the *Utility* when he was ten. At fifteen he sailed on the *Saxon* as a cook, under James Evans, master, and at twenty-two he was an able-seaman sailing in the *New Brunswick* and gaining very good reports throughout his career. Little did David know that both the *Utility* and the *New Brunswick* would eventually be wrecked.

In January 1878 a storm of great violence visited Morecambe Bay and the Fylde district generally, not unlike the near-hurricane that roared in on 11 November 1977, driving the seas before it to wreak chaos and roll far enough inland to batter in the front door of Mr Gornall's farmhouse at Winmarleigh, two miles away. America thoughtfully telegraphed a warning to Britain of the 1878 storm. 'Expect it about the 20th', they said, and sure enough it came. High and steady at 30.20, the mercury fell by Saturday to 29.50. Tides were the highest of the year. After a period of calm the gale, blowing strongly from the west, recommenced. Traditionally, such brief respites, well known to experienced mariners, were opportunities to batten down the hatches, 'eat a dead man's breakfast' and brace oneself for further onslaught.

Tugs escorting a three-masted sailing ship into Wyre Dock at the end of a long sea voyage in 1978, a year of severe gales.

The Bourne Arms at Knott End, haven for sailors shipwrecked on Pilling Sands.

All day Wednesday severe squalls and excessively heavy rain, aided by a bitter, fierce gale howling from seaward, sent heavy seas crashing all round Morecambe Bay. Chapel Street, Bonny Street and Lytham Road in Blackpool were all flooded and the oldest inhabitants declared it was many years since they had seen such a sea. Lytham's hulking was pierced opposite Lowther Gardens but St Annes, veiled in brown sand raging from the dunes, otherwise suffered little damage. Stiff-lipped and as well-bred as ever, the growing town might almost have been mistaken for a Sarahan oasis.

Out on Pilling Sands at the first light of day a schooner was discovered half a mile from the shore lighthouse at Fleetwood. The crew of the *Utility* had passed a fearful night. On her way to Belfast with coal she had been driven back by the force of the winds into Morecambe Bay. Her chains broken, her anchor parted and sails gone with the wind, the schooner had drifted onto Bernard's wharf where terrific seas continued to break over her. All her lights were doused and the crew's pathetic attempt to signal distress with torches passed unnoticed. As a last resource the four men lashed themselves to the rigging to brave the piercing cold and battering seas as well they might. For four hours, humping and lifting, the schooner finally dropped onto the sands off Preesall. The tide receded but the exhausted men, stiff with cold, could scarcely move. Helped by the other three, William Quinn, aged nineteen, finally managed to crawl to the Bourne Arms Hotel, but all attempts to save him by applying warmth and sustenance failed. The three older seamen survived the ordeal, but at the inquest on William and at the full Board of Trade Enquiry many questions were asked. Not only had the *Utility* no warning lights aboard, the Screw Pile lighthouse keepers had no means of warning those onshore that a vessel was in distress.

Alone at the mercy of the ocean, the mariner could use any luck that came his way, and he set great store by charms and customs. The infant born with a caul conferred safety on the grown sailor's voyaging. Any baby born at sea was credited with second sight. Extensive tattooing, the wearing of ear-rings, touching cold iron, avoiding whistling and the using of certain expressions whilst at sea all had great significance to sailors and fishermen. But how a schooner could have ventured forth in those perilous days without 'Old Blue Lights' first making adequate provision passes belief (George Laurie, a Fleetwood chemist, had attempted to patent his code of marine coloured lights, but went bankrupt). Henry Croft admitted that he had perceived faint torch signals but there were no rockets in readiness to fire from the lighthouse and warn those on shore.

More money to be spent on look-out duty on stormy nights and the provision of warning signals on board ship and at Wyre Lighthouse were sternly recommended. The long sermon preached at the special service for William Quinn provided the Reverend M. Shorrock with classic reference to life's stormy sea and the degree of preparedness all mankind needed to store up against hidden danger. He had a large, captive congregation in church that day, but the thoughts of the four men exposed to

Right: Some of the Croft brothers, ferrymen over the River Wyre. From back: John Croft, William Croft, R. Rawlinson, and Thomas Croft. (junior).

Below: The *Emily Warbrick*, one of the Wyre Shipping Co.'s vessels, was one of a fleet of thirty-seven ranging from 86 to 200 tons. She was built as a brigantine at Fleetwood in 1872, salted, 167 tons. She was converted into a three-mast topsail schooner and sailed with cargoes of china clay until being refitted as a cruising yacht. Renamed *Lost Horizon*, she was burned out returning from the West Indies.

the elements on the frail, disintegrating *Utility* amidst the darkness and din will never be known.

Ageing vessels there were in plenty, known to seasoned sailors as 'floating coffins'. A close study of wreck depositions for the 1870s up to the beginning of this century shows a remarkable number of wreckings by storms in the Irish Sea. Some victims were ships 'down on their luck'.

The loss of the *E. Shun* in January 1879 was deeply felt in Fleetwood, as she was acknowledged as a beauty. The story is told that when the first large vessel of this class moved off the stocks into the water the cry 'O how she scoons' went up in awed admiration. 'Very well, then let her be a schooner', said the builder, a Massachusetts man. *E. Shun* was three-masted and all went well with her voyage until 9 January at 1 a.m., ninety miles from Sandy Hook under double-reefed canvas as an east-south-east wind built up into a strong gale. Shipping a heavy sea over the stern, binnacle and compass were carried away and the cabin flooded. A temporary binnacle was fixed at latitude 39.30 N, longitude 58.50 W. The ship by now was steering east by south under close-reefed topsails when the enormous force of solid seas pooped the vessel, broke the wheel in two and carried away all gratings. From the south-west on 16 January came a hurricane at 2 p.m. when the schooner was running under close-reefed stay sail, shifting at 10 p.m. to north-east, which caused a tremendous sea to strike the vessel's stern, breaking her rudder at the lower end of the case, carrying away steering blocks and sweeping men's feet from under them. A degree of tiredness beyond most people's understanding had settled on the crew, trying to catch commands snatched away by the whining, roaring wind. The crew could not relax for a moment. One big sea into the hatch way would have sent her to the bottom, so they hung on to the billowing hatch tarpaulins, bodies crusted with salt, as were beards, eyes and noses. On the 18th the weather moderated and the crew managed to steer her by hoving chain through the shackel of the after-side rudder. Unremitting, 5 February sent a west-north-west hurricane, running yet another tremendous sea. Samuel Randall and R.C. Dill were washed overboard and drowned. The same sea took the fore skylight, smashed both boats, broke through the stanchions of poop rail and did even more serious damage to the rudder, which completely gave up the ghost at 10 p.m. On the 14th they tried to wear the ship with drogues and cut away the mizzen mast. Between the 11th and 21st the Fleetwood vessel was quite unmanageable. With what joy they hailed the German schooner *Cadet*, which took off all the crew and set the *E. Shun* on fire so that she was not a danger to other shipping.

On 11 and 12 November 1879, in a very severe gale, one of the oldest trading schooners, the *Ann Shephered*, under Captain Jones of Liverpool, broke her anchor and drifted with the tide, smashing against the wall of Clarence Dock. The crew climbed onto the ends of the masts and jumped onto the warehouses. As she was not insured she became a 'dead loss'. In the same storm the screw steamer *Thistle* was damaged off Walney Island but towed in by Captain Roskell.

Mississippi, moored in the centre, had a gross tonnage of 2,159, length 320ft.

On the right of the photograph, *Leven* looks dwarfed, moored at Liverpool near the huge steamer *Illinois*. The *Leven* was sunk off Blackpool on 20 October 1873. The lifeboat *Robert William* reached two of her crew.

A task worthy of the labour of Hercules occurred on 4 September 1879. The wind, blowing from the south-west all day, increased to gale in the evening. The schooner *Elizabeth Ellen Fisher*, under Captain Wright, parted her cable and was blown on Bernard's Wharf. A second anchor let go also broke, and she grounded, but not being stuck fast in sand, received an even worse battering. 187 tons of pig-iron cargo from Ardrossan shifted. Captain Stirzaker attempted to tow the lifeboat by tug but the rope broke. Maroons were fired for more lifeboat crew under coxswain Robert Wright and soldiers of the 36th Regiment at Euston Barrack rushed out in a body with ropes to help launch the lifeboat which had been pitched off the stocks with such force it got stuck in sand. Straining every sinew, the men lifted the lifeboat bodily to the water's edge but at the expense of long delay. By 5 a.m. Captain Roskell with the *Columbus* had preceded to the schooner but could not approach the breaking surf. From the Lower Lighthouse a large crowd anxiously watched the efforts to get near the schooner in a sea running mountains high. Eventually the crew of four were rescued, with *Columbus* standing by, at 7.40 a.m. Bruised and weary, the lifeboatmen ate an excellent breakfast at the home of Mr Fisher, the owner of the vessel which was not insured, but some of her cargo was rescued.

Just as the crew of the *Elizabeth Ellen Fisher* was landed at Ferryslip, Captain Cross of the *Duke of Connaught* arrived with a crew of twelve hands from the barque *Thilda*, picked up six miles from Duddon Banks. Captain Niels Hultgren had set off for Norway from Liverpool in tow of the Russian boat *Cronstadt* with a cargo of salt when the gale took the foretop, mast and main topgallant of his 463-ton barque, leaving only her mizzen stay sail. The captain flashed signals and burned flare lights all night until, at 5 a.m. on Friday, the *Duke of Connaught* steamer hove in sight, whereupon the wrecked crew set sail for her in a punt. The barque had by now 7ft of water in her hold. The crew were all Norwegians except for a Negro cook, who nearly drowned as the punt capsized. So eager was the latter, he seized the steward by his teeth and, once on board the steamer, was overwhelming in his thanks. An unidentified barque was also sunk in Morecambe Bay on Wednesday 3 September 1879. Fishermen reported its masts discernible, sunk four miles south of Morecambe lightship.

Gibson's Shipyard of Fleetwood had the job of overhauling and re-decking the *Thomas Bell* of Liverpool. In a great storm, travelling from San Francisco in February 1879, to use a sailor's expression, her 'decks were cleared'. It cost £800 to refit her in Wyre Dock, the work being undertaken not long after the death of John Gibson, who had started the firm. The full-rigged ship *Glen Lyon*, also from San Francisco, with 1,000 tons of wheat, managed to reach Fleetwood with only minor damage. There was now a busy grain trade at Wyre Dock with so much traffic that ships had to wait for the signalling flag, the *Halcyon*, a 1,840-ton screw steamer, being the largest ever to enter. New warehouses were erected but the dock entrance was already proving too narrow. The last year of a decade or century often did its worst where storms were concerned, and 1879 was no exception. Rough seas of February crippled the *Lord Howe*, and Captain Emundson's vessel, No.67140 of Fleetwood, which sailed with coal, was posted missing at Lloyds on 26 February. A serious accident occurred on 16 December 1879 when the North Lancashire Steam Navigation Co.'s mail steamer *Thomas Dugdale*, commanded by Captain Brown, with her anchor cable broken, drifted helplessly and blocked the entrance to Wyre Dock. As she was filling with water, a tug took off her passengers. With her stern under water and her bows up in the air, it was feared she might break her back. Crowds watched from the shore whilst cargo, including livestock, was removed and workmen were hurried out to repair the gash in her side. The tugs *Nelson* and *Wyre* eventually got the *Thomas Dugdale* off the sandbank and she was towed away to Barrow for repair. To a lesser extent the same happened to another mail steamer, the *Earl of Ulster*, on the following day. This anchor cable snapping was blamed on extremely frosty weather, which in its way could also create chaos.

Northfleet, an inshore craft, dredged up this huge 12ft anchor from the seabed during a fishing trip off Nelson, near Southport, late summer 1980. Its great age is pronounced by the wooden stock and it is probably from a sailing schooner. The Morecambe Bay Chart indicated 'wreck' close to where it was found. James Robertson & Son hauled it into Jubilee Quay and the Local Historical Society put it on show. Dave Smith and trawlerman John Donough are examining the find.

The police of Fleetwood were notified of the total wreck of the *Janet Wignall*, with the loss of all hands on the Scottish coast on 20 January 1879. The vessel was under the command of Captain Jones and was in passage from Liverpool to Creetown in ballast when she stranded in the parish of Bargue, near Dumfries. Three farm servants passing along the shore on the Sunday observed pieces of wreckage under high rocks. At once they started searching and discovered five bodies. The managing owner at Fleetwood, Mr Wignall, said there would not be more than seven persons on board and probably all had drowned. The schooner, which was a total wreck, had traded for several years on that route. The crew were John Cooper (mate), James Blackley, Abel Williams and John Eastwood. The passengers were John Cochran and John Broady, a well-known dwarf who, with Cochran, had been visiting Liverpool and got a passage home. The scene of the wreck was reported as a terrible place, some of the cliffs rising perpendicular to a height of 95ft, the country of Scott's novel *Guy Mannering*. The mangled

A Mediterranean water carrier dredged up by the *Bleasdale* in 1968, near Lune deeps. In perfect condition, it probably fell overboard from one of the barquentines of the nineteenth century, or came from a wreck.

Empress Queen.

British Prince.

bodies of the drowned men had to be hoisted to the top of the cliff. All were buried in the local churchyard by the sea, their coffins bearing emblems of the Odd Fellows and Foresters' Societies to which some of the dead belonged, draped with Union Jacks.

Another schooner, the *Kate* of Fleetwood, suffered on 2 October 1879. Thomas O. Rowlands witnessed on Oath that dense fog brought on the disaster. The schooner was travelling under plain sail, lights properly fitted in the fore rigging and burning clear, with a good look-out on duty, when a steamer whistle was heard two points on the starboard bow, and they kept their course, thinking it was proceeding down channel, but directly the steamer, lights blazing, struck them amidships on the starboard side, cutting the vessel to the main hatch. All hands immediately got on board the steamer (as *Kate* was doomed to founder), which proved to be the tug *Stormcock* of Liverpool. A dense fog had prevailed for two days and their speed was maintained at three knots.

It is strange that some ships seem to have been lucky or unlucky from the day they were launched. Whereas a landsman might look on a series of misfortunes as mere chance, sailors heeded curses and believed that some ships were 'hoodoo'd'. Women who lost their husbands or sons might well curse the ship responsible, and it was not always easy to get a crew together if this happened. The notion of phantom ships was widely held, the belief being that these were vessels that had gone down and, as wraiths, were trying to find their homeport. Some sailors averred they had seen these ghost wrecks, manned by the spirits of their lost crews, groping through the mist and

Celtic.

Scythia.

making for familiar moorings. It is understandable, for clouds disturbed by wind and waves take strange shapes and, aided by fear, hunger and fatigue, a man at the whim of the elements, knowing he hovers between life and death, could be convinced. Scientific explanation did not interest the seasoned sailor. He believed that the souls of doomed sailors entered the bodies of sea birds, that should one bird come day by day and alight on the vessel, it was a warning of impending disaster. He even believed that in times of great stress his drowned mate came back to help, giving him the strength of two men, which he certainly needed at the height of a storm.

As for the wrecks, men have been fascinated by the hulks of sunken ships for centuries. Every wrecked ship belongs to someone, for, should ownership not be traced it is vested in the Crown. The days when the seven seas were criss-crossed by sailing ships which harmonised to perfection with the clouds and the flying spume, like gulls fitting into any sea setting, are gone, and it is sadly ironic that as little as £10 can buy a wreck. As with rotting piers, owners have been glad to give them away. Names like *Traver, Good Intent, Crusader, Mary Scott, Brooklyn, Ocean Monarch, Hope, Sovereign of the Seas, Parthia, Persian, Mary Rosanna* and *Flying Cloud* ring down the years. One wonders, will there ever be anything to compare with the primal power of ship versus the elements, to stir the blood and play on the full range of human emotions. It is doubtful, but not surprising, for man set sail long before he sat on a horse or trudged behind a wheel.

There were occasions at Southport when high tides flowed down Lord Street. This historic photograph from 1870 proves the point. The *Visitor Newspaper* reported the epic voyage of the steamship *Cambria*, owned by the Southport Steamship Co. Ltd, when the lives of seventy people were in danger. On the return journey from New Brighton at 6.30 p.m. 'All went well until passing through the Formby Channel when a terrific squall of rain and wind broke over the boat. Wind and rain so increased in violence that the captain decided to make for Liverpool, but this, too, proved unsafe and he had to make for the open sea. Passengers, especially the ladies, were in a state of terror.'

A long list of pleasure ships sailed from Southport. *Belle*, *Wellington*, *Greyhound*, *Deerhound*, *Lady Margaret* and *Queen of the Bay*, which sooner or later encountered stormy seas. The Channel, Bull's Run and Birkdale Channel made approach to the pier possible, which until 1936 was always surrounded by fishing boats and yachts and visiting paddle steamers such as the *Emperor* from Bournemouth, which made a special trip on 2 August 1928 in calmer, summer seas.

The year 1808 reported 'Many disasters amongst the shipping along the coast and 1833 saw one of the most severe storms ever witnessed. The hurricane-force winds lasted five hours and many vessels were wrecked'. In 1888 the barque *Albert Williams*

Southport's famous and fashionable Lord Street severely flooded by storms in the 1850s.

Southport's lifeboat in 1897 in one of the Irish Sea's fiercest storms.

A view of Southport in 1897.

A fishing vessel which came to grief off Burbo Sandbanks. Sea charts as early as 1801 warned of the shifting nature of sandbanks which could, within a week, alter a good channel.

This fishing vessel was over 100 years old. Whatever could be salvaged, spars, ropes and sails were carted off by horses. 'Wrecke and wayfe of the sea' had been a bone of contention for centuries. At the time of this photograph 100 fishing vessels had been reduced in number because of the silting at Southport, but fishing smacks could sail from the pier until the 1930s.

was wrecked but later re-floated. The work of unloading her 5,000 bags of grain then proceeded, but proved so arduous that one horse dropped dead and two were lost in the Bog Hole. Marshside fishermen carted the bags to Southport Railway Station.

In the early nineteenth century, North Meols men, Robert, Thomas and William Rimmer and William and Joseph Crompton were charged with stealing 1 cwt of cotton from the wrecked brigantine *Lascelles*.

One of the most famous Southport lifeboatmen was William Bibby who 'rescued 400 persons from a watery grave'. He was not among the Southport crew on the night of the *Mexico* disaster, but he was involved in the repair of the *Mexico* when she was taken to Lytham. The *Mexico*, finally lost in the Bay of Biscay, was involved in the worst lifeboat disaster that ever occurred, in 1886, for two crews perished from the lifeboats that set out. The wreck had a cargo of machetes, and to this day Southport has examples of them, gruesome reminders of that tragedy.

Above: Emperor, 2 August 1928.

Right: Lifeboatman John Aindow, Formby (near Liverpool).

Below: William Bibby.

6

LIFEBOATS OUT

The last twenty years of the nineteenth century can veritably be described as wreck-packed, so many blind, bewildered ships fell victim to wind and tide. They include some of the most dramatic incidents and the worst ever lifeboat disaster.

9 January 1880 brought news of the shattered wreck of the Fleetwood schooner *Robert Drape*. On 10 February, when gales wrought havoc on the west coast, a collision between the *Earl of Ulster* and the *City of Tanjore* occurred in the River Wyre; the schooner *E.E. Fisher* was forced aground, but it was later found possible to make her fit for sea again.

Not so with the *Bessie Jones*, a Fleetwood vessel carrying 200 tons of old iron rails. A west-north-west gale had blown her onto the west side of Salthouse Bank about three miles off Blackpool. Here she was descried at 6.30 a.m., but the alarm was not raised for an hour. Hauled out of the Lytham Road boathouse, the *Robert William* was launched from South Pier at 8.20 a.m., crewed by Robert Bickerstaffe, coxswain; John Parkinson, bowman; James Swarbrick; William Rimmer; J.T. Fish; Richard Fish; John Fish; F. Owen; J. Wiley; John Stanhope and Richard Parkinson – two men short, but no more precious time could be wasted. It was impossible to use oars against the huge waves breaking on the shore. To get through the boiling surf, sails were hoisted, although this was against the rules, but Bickerstaffe gauged that two single-reefed sails would achieve what was necessary. His judgement was precise, and once away the crew lowered sail, took oars and after battling for two and a half hours found themselves alongside the wreck. Spars and all manner of wreckage hampered the work of reaching the crew who were clustered in the rigging, battling for their lives.

Sheared up to the vessel and made fast with grappling irons, the lifeboat was in considerable danger, frequently banged by the helpless *Bessie Jones*. One man had been lost during the morning wait and the other four, lashed to the rigging, were numb with cold. A line was thrown, and in this way Captain Pater and his men were rescued. A dangerous return journey then had to be braved, during which the fury of the sea set the *Robert William* on her beam ends, flinging out J.T. Fish, who, by a miracle, was washed back into the boat on another wave.

Left: Fleetwood skippers Philip Kay and Jack Dyer, 1888.

Below: The first St Annes lifeboat in the nineteenth century, with Laura Janet and crew. (By permission of Lytham St Annes Lifeboat Service)

The new Lytham St Annes lifeboat in new lifeboat house, 2007. (Courtesy of Patrick Ramsey)

Old Lytham lifeboat house and windmill. (Courtesy of Patrick Ramsey)

Above and below: Ships' anchors from the days of sailing found on Lytham Beach.

Landing at Blackpool was out of the question and the storm-tossed lifeboat made for St Annes, where a wildly cheering crowd had gathered to greet its victorious return. The *Bessie Jones*, 230 tons burden, 114 tons register and registered A1 at Lloyds, was six years old, having been built at Barnstaple, North Devon. Samuel Laycock wrote a poem about his friend J.T. Fish in the Lancashire dialect, of which he was a master.

Incident followed incident throughout the years 1880-1881. On 10 March 1880 the fishing smack *Prince Charlie* of Fleetwood struck ground and sank, though she was raised later and tugged in for repairs. Also in March, Fleetwood brigantine *Chalciope* was in collision with the *Conway* in the River Mersey. The brig was brought to Fleetwood for repairing at Gibson's Shipyard. In the following month a new pilot boat, the *Albicore*, was launched by Miss Jenny Hesketh to cope with increased traffic in the Wyre and reduce accidents, but two vessels, *Strossmeyer* and *Llodd*, went aground in the estuary of the Wyre on 4 June.

On 29 October 1880 a great storm struck Morecambe Bay, particularly severe off the Isle of Man. The 150-ton, two-masted schooner *Janet Hughes* of Caernarvon had been seen drifting past the Morecambe Bay lightship at the height of the storm. *Edward Wasey* lifeboat was launched from Fleetwood under coxswain Robert Wright and bowman Fred Bettes to aid the distressed vessel, which was later towed to Barrow and saved from total wreck.

February 1881. The steamer Thomas Dugdale collided with the *Doris* and sank her. In the same month a record was set up by the Fleetwood-bound barque *Archibald Fuller*, from San Francisco. She left on 12 June 1880 with a cargo of wheat and arrived in the 'extraordinary period of eight months and three days... a most remarkable record for which Captain Kite was presented with the bear flag for push and energy.'

John Jones, master of the barque *C.P.D.*, 1,106 tons, which left Iquique for Hamburg on 5 October with 1,630 tons of nitrate of soda on board, ran into a north-west gale in January, veering south-west with terrific squalls and a high cross-sea running. At 4 a.m. on 27 January they shipped a heavy sea over starboard which washed away the bulwarks, poop, binnacle and compass, but they managed to reach Fleetwood by February, where an account was given of how many gales in the course of a long voyage had erupted, and at what cost. This was made at the Custom House and placed in the Wreck Deposition Register.

May 1881. An enquiry was held into the grounding of the *Estella* on Mort Flats, Morecambe Bay, where she had sprung a leak. Despite adverse weather, the accident could have been prevented had the master used his lead judiciously for soundings.

June 1881. The schooner *Margaret* of Fleetwood, under Captain Close, became a total wreck after being run down in thick weather in the Mersey. She was built at Ardrossan in 1867 by Hugh Barclay, a 90-ton schooner rigged with two masts. As the screw steamer *Puno*, belonging to the Pacific Steam Navigation Co., struck, the *Margaret* went down immediately with only five hands escaping.

Fleetwood Watch House, built in 1839.

The stranding of the paddle steamer *Earl of Ulster* at Jurby Point occurred in March 1881. Schooner-rigged, 644 tons, the Fleetwood vessel was commanded by Leonard Humphreys, carrying general merchandise and travelling across the Irish Sea from Belfast to Fleetwood. They experienced a heavy sea with showers of sleet, the wind increasing in strength until, by the time the *Copeland* was found, a whole gale from the south-east was striking. Even so, they kept on full speed. On the 4th, on the starboard bow, a sea struck, stoving in the starboard bridge boat, breaking part of the rail and stanchions and a portion of the boat's chocks. A light on the starboard beam was taken to be the Point of Ayr, but whilst the master, who had been stunned, was resting from the shock, leaving the first mate in charge, the latter came running with the cry 'Ship's aground'.

The vessel remained perfectly upright in calm water, and daylight revealed that they were ashore near Jurby Point, Isle of Man. Luckily the ship floated about 10.15 a.m., when the crew, sounding the pumps and finding no water, proceeded with caution to Fleetwood, where they arrived at the Screw Pile lighthouse at about 6 p.m., the pumps being sounded every half hour. The casualty occurred by mistaking the light seen for the Point of Ayr, which, according to the length of passage and position, the master believed it to be.

20 October 1881. The *Iron King* from Liverpool arrived at Douglas Harbour, her master's job having been to tow the barque *Lebu*, light with ballast, from Maryport

to Cardiff. A gale struck from the south-east and the tug, making water, had to abandon *Lebu* and set course for Douglas Harbour with a report of what had occurred. The barque, left to the full fury of one of the worst gales in memory, sent up signals of distress, seen by the lifeboat *John Turner-Turner*. Manned by a crew of eighteen, they attempted to tack to the *Lebu*, but the gale was so strong that the men became exhausted. A second lifeboat, *Manchester*, and *Salford Sunday Schools*, put out to take off the crew of the barque, but on the return journey capsized, and although it righted itself, eleven men were drowned (four lifeboatmen, the captain and six sailors of the *Lebu*). A large sum was collected for the widows and orphans.

In November 1881, the barquentine *Saxon*, with 153 tons of china clay, struck a hurricane (north-west gale force 12). The *Vindolanda*, a schooner, grounded near Wyre Dock on 22 November. These November gales washed flotsam and jetsam all along the coast. At Blackpool wreckage described as 'barrels of syrupy liquid having the smell of rum' was secured by police officers, but private individuals found and hid some of the barrels which originated from a vessel stranded off Formby. (According to very recent evidence it was Formby that had the first lifeboat of all on the British coasts – ten years before Bamburgh.)

St Peter's Church, Quernmore, was reported in the 1881 Directory of Lancaster as having a three-light east window, rescued from a ship which was wrecked on its way to Cannes. W.J. Garnett of Quernmore Park purchased it for the church at the wreck sale, the subjects of the medallions in the three lights being the nativity, the crucifixion and the resurrection.

Formby Lifeboat near Southport.

6 January 1882. The *Fleetwood Chronicle* reported the loss of the fishing boat *Mary Ellen* with all her crew of five, one of the most serious disasters that ever befell the local fleet.

February 1882. *Englishman* and *Knottladen* went aground in the Wyre. The barque *Venus* of Sweden was struck by disastrous seas, but the lifeboat managed to save her crew of twelve.

March 1882. *Lady Dufferin*, *Fawn* and *Pride* were completely wrecked at a time when there was strong feeling in Fleetwood about the Blackpool paddle steamer *Dhu Artach* being converted to a steam trawler. The smacks men feared for their livelihood and made such a fuss that the idea had to be given up.

The storms sweeping over Lancashire that February ranked among the most memorable 'atmospheric disturbances' within the life-spans of the oldest inhabitants. Rising rapidly on Thursday night, the wind raged with such unsurpassed fury that sleep was impossible. Many occupants never went to bed at all, knowing that the seas would sweep over the front, flood streets and put them in double-danger from both wind and water. Chimney pots, lead, tiles, bricks, walls and shutters were dislodged by the terrible power of the gale, which blew in windows and ripped away tradesmen's signboards. John Worthington's new Coffee House at South Shore, three storeys high and incomplete, was razed to the ground. The wall of the Fleetwood Grain Elevator facing the river was severely cracked for 25ft. Also at Fleetwood, large quantities of bacon were washed up. Although the Customs authorities took charge of all they

Steam trawler *Doris* FD141 in Lune Deeps.

Fleetwood Dock, 1902.

could find, many sides were seized by the soldiers at the Hutment Barracks, to be quickly roasted and eaten before the commanding officer could intervene. Part of the cargo of the *City* of Brussels, wrecked at the mouth of the Mersey, when sold privately this prime bacon fetched 12/6*d* a cwt. Other plunder – flour, butter and lard – continued to be washed up as far as Blackpool, and there were a number of incidents in which people ruined their best clothes scuffling for the unusual sea harvest. Eventually it was thought wise to send the bell man round, warning that in the interest of health the unfit food should not be eaten.

That wild night those on board the steamer *Eden*, which had sailed from Fleetwood, were signalled that assistance was at hand. Robert Wright decided to launch the *Child of Hale*, and soon the *Fylde* was steaming down harbour with the lifeboat in tow. At about 11 a.m. the watchers on shore saw the signal rocket fired by Coastguard Dougherty and knew that the lifeboat had arrived. It was discovered that the vessel's crew had got on the banks at Sunderland Point, when both her cables had parted. With the lifeboat showing the way, she was piloted before the gale into Glasson Dock.

The Norwegian barque *Adelgrunde*, making for Fleetwood, took the ground near the Landmark, and the combined efforts of harbour tugs *Fylde* and *Wyre* could not move her. Captain Hansen stoutly maintained he had been led astray by changes made in the neighbourhood with the buoys. The vessel had left Liverpool on the previous Tuesday for Halifax, Nova Scotia, with 500 tons of salt on board as bal-

Mona's Queen in Fleetwood, 1890. Note the cannon on the sea wall.

last. All the sails were blown away, the drinking water spoiled, the crew exhausted and the mate had his arm broken. The captain, with repairs in mind, had run for Fleetwood, and it was then that his vessel stranded. Deeply embedded in sand, almost on her beam ends, with rudder broken off, seams opened and cargo washed away, she became a total wreck. It was fortunate that the *Adelgrunde* was fully insured.

The Allan Line and Dominion Line in 1883 were still transporting emigrants at special low rates (saloon 10 guineas, steerage 4 guineas) from Liverpool to USA and Canada. Both advertised regularly 'Assisted ocean rates for agricultural labourers, their families, female domestics £3 per adult, mechanics, navvies, general labourers and their families. Children under 12 years £2, infants under one 10/-'. Flynn & Main of James Street provided a map of Manitoba and the Canadian Pacific Railway. The Allan Line ships included *Caspian*, *Grecian*, *Parisian*, *Nova Scotian*, *Sarmatian*, *Prussian*, *Peruvian*, *Austrian*, *Hibernian*, *Circassian* and *Polynesian*. Through tickets at special rates to Chicago, Winnipeg and north-west territories could lead to a new and prosperous lease of life, but rough, dangerous crossings meant that countless hopefuls never arrived. 'Presumed lost' was posted up when the ship became long overdue. Tell-tale wreckage was sometimes found months or years later, sighted by passing ships or washed up on distant shores.

Flotsam and jetsam, sport of the sea, handed over to the Receiver of Wreck, ended up in wreck sales. Mr Poole of Fleetwood, on 8 June 1883, sold by auction a rowing boat picked up at sea by the Fleetwood pilot cutter. It was bought by Mr J. Bradshaw for £3-10-0. Three life buoys were sold for 12/-, and a large meat safe for the same sum. The previous month, wreckage from the iron steamer *Mercury* was auctioned by Mr W. Langley as it lay on Blackpool beach, comprising iron hull, partially broken to pieces, engine and screw propeller, upright tubular boiler, steam winch, ship's pump, two anchors and chain cable.

In March of the same year soldiers trying to walk out to the wreck of the barque *Adelgrunde* got into difficulties on North Wharf, but luckily were seen by Coastguard Charles Dougherty, who raised the alarm. By the time the terrified trio were helped off the sandbank, the flood tide had reached waist high.

In September 1883 the schooner *Thornton* was wrecked in a gale off Fleetwood and sank. Gales that month damaged shipping in Morecambe Bay, including *Sir Robert Peel*, *Onward*, *Big Petrel* and *Oyster Girl*. A fisherman was swept overboard from the *Emblem*. *Ezra*, *Comet* and *Margaret Agnes* were also wrecked in November 1883.

The wreck of the barque *Mermaid* on the morning of Thursday 11 December 1883 led to a poem by Minnie Wormald of Southport praising the lifeboat which saved all hands.

On 27 January 1884 the brigantine *Bgannisan* of 440 tons, laden with cotton, on voyage from Charlestown to Liverpool, became a total wreck on Horse Bank, off Lytham. The crew gave no signal of their whereabouts, and by early morning light were taken off by the Southport lifeboat. Meanwhile, Lytham's lifeboat had put out, and that of St Annes was damaged attempting a launch.

In February 1884 news arrived in Fleetwood that wreckage of the *Ellen Widdup* had been sighted. *Woodbine* and *Anne Walker*, less damaged, were sold for £120 and £150 respectively. The first week was one of the stormiest ever, with fishing smacks struggling through, facing disaster, to get fish to the populace. Gales on the Saturday were of terrific violence, and with the barometer falling rapidly much disturbance was expected ahead. High water coincided with the most violent of winds, forcing seas of immense volume over promenades and up streets.

One of Mr Porter's fleet, the *Lizzie Porter*, under Captain Hesketh, had set sail on 1 November from Curaçao. In the squally voyage that followed they lost main gaff, foremast, jib-boom and topsail. Crew cut away gear which, in falling, broke stanchions, rails, bulwarks and the jolly boat. Repairs having been obtained at Vigo, they proceeded to sea on 20 January, but by the 26th the wind increased, carrying away mizzen, rigging and mast. Huge seas began to breach her; the vessel filled and was thrown broadside on the rocks of an uninhabited island off the French coast. The crew of eight, finding what shelter they could, existed on provisions washed up from the wreck until rescued and sent by the British Consul home to Fleetwood via St Malo to tell all about the roughest passage of their careers.

In March 1884 *Ethel Gwendoline* was wrecked in the long ridge of Mort Flats, 7½ miles from Wyre Light. The master, Mr Bryant, who had reported that afternoon,

Mr Porter's fleet, Fleetwood, 1900s.

set off to Fowey with a load of china clay. On foundering, he and the crew landed back in Fleetwood in the ship's boat. Examining the wreck from the ferry steamer *Success*, Fred Carter, the agent, found all hatches open, a hole in the bottom and the cargo spoiled. All movables (tarpaulins, stores, wheels, blocks, utensils) were taken off. Liverpool Salvage Association went out to the wrecked steamer and decided it was worth saving.

An example of the speed of turnabout expected from cargo boats is instanced by the SS *Dungormel* of Belfast arriving with 360 tons of iron ore in March 1884. She docked at noon, commenced discharge at 1 p.m. and by 4.30 p.m. was clear, with 360 tons of coal loaded, ready to leave on the midnight tide from Wyre Dock.

May 1884. The barque *Mary and Anne* was wrecked off Southport. She had left Drogheda on the Monday, travelling to Liverpool. Rough weather carried away both her masts and she drifted towards Southport. The vessel became a total wreck, but the lifeboat came alongside and rescued the crew.

September 1884. Storms damaged the Blackpool pleasure steamer *Bickerstaffe* and revived memories of 20 May 1880, when the pleasure paddle steamer *Columbus*, cruising from Liverpool and loaded with passengers, grounded 150 yards from the North Pier jetty in Blackpool. The sea broke over her, and the passengers, although in no real danger, were terrified to see the flag of distress hoisted. The *Robert William* lifeboat, assisted by fishing smacks of the old Sailing Boat Co., brought off 133 passengers.

In the *Robert William*'s last great year of rescue she gave assistance to the barque *Madeira* of Savannah, off Norbreck, after which she went out only three times more. On 27 March she attended the barque *Medora* of Lerwick, and on 21 August 1882, the barque *Arethusa*, a vessel of 400 tons bound from Liverpool to Quebec. Ten men were saved from this vessel wrecked off Little Bispham, which went ashore through the drunken state of captain and crew. Finally on 13 December 1883 *Robert William* aided the barque *Mermaid* of Cardiff. Thus, after a great career of twenty years, during which she saved eighty-four lives, on 29 September 1885 the *Robert William* was replaced by the *Samuel Fletcher*, a day full of pageantry which attempted to show how much the lifeboat service and the men who made it possible were appreciated.

Monday 15 June 1885 was a happy occasion in St Annes, with the ceremonial launching of their lifeboat *Laura Janet* by Mrs Chadwick at the same time as the opening of St Annes Pier. Flags, bands, bunting and 3,000 visitors marked the occasion, with the Lytham, Blackpool, Southport and Fleetwood lifeboats lined up on display.

But the year had its sadness too. The London & North Western Railway Co.'s steamship *Admiral Moorsom*, built in 1860 by Randolph Elder & Co., had to be written off. Leaving Holyhead in 15 January 1885 with thirty-five passengers and a cargo of livestock, she met another steamer in the Irish Sea soon after 8 p.m. Rapidly altering course to keep clear, she passed the stern of this steamship only to be run down by the American steamer *Santa Clara*. Port paddle box, masts and funnel of *Admiral Moorsom* were carried away and all port boats smashed. Captain Weeks fell overboard and was lost. Eleven were picked up by the *Norwegian*, fourteen by the *Santa Clara*. The *Admiral Moorsom* was found at Arklow with five people still alive on board. September witnessed another collision, this time between fishing smacks *Industry* and *Dotterel*. The *Dotterel* was built at Freckleton in 1869, 55ft long, owned by William and Thomas Leadbetter, fish salesmen. She foundered in Lune Deeps.

November 1886. The sloop *Pennington* was wrecked sailing out of Liverpool. The Fleetwood lifeboat saved two lives. They also, in the same month, saved two from the Norwegian brig *Olga* and ten from the barque *Ruth Topping*, the *John Turner-Turner* lifeboat under 'Boxer' Corlett, the coxswain, rescued two from the smack *Alice* off Peel, Isle of Man.

One hundred years ago, when lifeboats were propelled by sails and oars, when barques, brigantines and schooners plied the sea-lanes, startling and thrilling incidents relating to the sea frequently made headline news for our island race. Momentarily stirred by eye-witness accounts and first-hand reports from survivors, people from inland towns praised to the skies the gallantry of lifeboat crews. Some dug deeply into their pockets for contributions, but in the welter of other events, typically it was soon forgotten.

The inauguration of Lifeboat Sundays and Saturdays was the first practical step to make the RNLI better known, and we can be proud that Lancashire businessman

William Leadbetter, lifeboatman and sailor.

Coxswain David Leadbetter, 1895.

Charles W. Macara took the initiative. From his holiday residence at St Annes he could see many a wreck on Horse Bank. He loved to escape from Manchester, and he grew to know the fishermen of St Annes very well.

The Fylde coastal towns needed no alerting to the dire necessity of supporting the Lifeboat Institution, for they witnessed the saving of lives and hundreds of thousands of pounds-worth of merchandise. They lived out the tense hours of the storms, especially those families whose men folk crewed the lifeboats. It was typical, too, that as the fortunes of the RNLI ebbed, some disaster would occur, demonstrating the heroism and self-denial of these fishermen. Such tragedies gave an impetus to much-needed funds and sharply alerted the nation to the ever-present dangers of the sea.

Considering the risks, the record of crewmen lost was marvellously small, but a Lancashire disaster of such proportions occurred in 1886 that it eclipsed everything previously recorded in the sixty-two years of the RNLI's existence. People were so moved by its stark heroism that within a fortnight £33,000 was collected. The German Emperor Wilhelm I sent £250, and incisive reporting by the *Yorkshire Post* and Sheffield *Daily Telegraph* raised a further £3,500 and £ 1,400 respectively.

In a bid to save the crew of the *Mexico*, bound from Hamburg to Liverpool, three lifeboats set off from the Lancashire coast in a storm of exceptional fury on the night of 9 December 1886. Southport, Lytham and St Annes all responded to the *Mexico*'s distress signals. Rockets sent up from the lighthouse summoned the scattered crew of thirteen, eight of whom were ready as the *Laura Janet* was run out of the boathouse. Four volunteers stepped forward; Coxswain William Johnson came dashing up at the last minute to take charge, and onlookers noticed that the magnitude of the task was summed up in the grave expression of experienced sub-coxswain Charles Tims.

The St Annes lifeboat left at 10.30 p.m., but many of the crowd who wished her 'God speed' waited anxiously on the shore all night. Some went to Mr Macara's house for reassurance, only to be met by the terrible news that bodies of lifeboatmen had been cast up on the opposite shore. Whose? Hours later the Lytham lifeboat was sighted, and so anxious was the agonised crowd of relatives waiting helplessly onshore, a horseman rode into the waves to meet it on their behalf. He returned with the appalling announcement that of three boats only one had returned. Thirteen of the crew of fifteen had been lost from the Southport boat and every man from the St Annes boat, both having capsized. (In May 1887 the statue of a lifeboatman was unveiled on St Annes seafront, and part of the proceedings was the launching of a new lifeboat appropriately named *The Brothers*.) So it fell to the lot of the *Charles Biggs*, with coxswain, gallant old Tom Clarkson, to rescue the twelve men from the *Mexico*. On that wild night RNLI secretary, Mr C.A. Myers, and Mr H.H. Harrison, had been on the beach, seen the signals of distress and raised the alarm. Coxswain Clarkson at the inquiry into the disaster gave evidence:

Lytham St Annes statue commemorating the worst lifeboat disaster ever in the history of the RNLI. Two lifeboats were lost rescuing the *Mexico*. (Courtesy of Patrick Ramsey)

As we approached the wreck the water broke and four or five times the boat was full. I called out to the men to take the masts and sails down ... the sea gave us a lurch and we broke four oars, the boat partly on her beam ends made for the ship with her shoulder to the waves. When we got to the Mexico the Captain threw a black box to the lifeboat, the ship's papers, but it went into the water. One of the crew caught hold of a rope to lower himself. We caught hold and lugged him in head first. We got them all off. The Captain lowered himself last with a rope made fast round him. He was an elderly man. We could see a big crowd gathered on shore and burning lights. What were we going to do in a sea like that? We let her drift, but she did not do exactly to my liking so I turned her back. We put her on the port tack and a tremendous sea smacked over us. The Captain said, 'We have a very good boat'. As we passed Southport pier I said to the Captain, 'Will you come with us or go ashore here?'

'Where you go I will go,' was his reply. So we made straight for Lytham and got home about half past three in the morning, all of us wet through and half drowned.

What a first assignment that was for a new lifeboat!

In Southport to this day are machetes, taken from the wreck which also washed up near Guides House, off Warton Bank, cement in barrels, which hardened and broke the staves. These were laid in three tiers but are now hidden with slutch, mud and shingle. The Local History Society has discussed unearthing them to re-live the drama of the *Mexico*.

Storms in 1886 were described by Miss Hannah Rossall of Pilling, an old inhabitant, as 'the worst I remember. The tide came over the bridge and down the hill towards the mill. The storm came in the night and my father had ropes over our house and my brothers and sisters and I had to hang on to the ropes to keep the roof on.' The dome of Pilling Mill was blown off into Jackson's fields. Its sails had been removed earlier and taken to Binks Farm, Eagland Hill, to be used as gate posts. Three vessels were forced onto Fluke Hall sands and wrecked. On 7 January Mr Barton of the Bourne Arms Hotel, Knott End, got a horse and cart ready, setting off with men to the ketch *Swallow*, fast on Pilling Sands, where they found the body of Thomas Rimmer hanging from the rigging, dead from exposure and mutilation. His dangling watch had stopped at ten minutes to twelve. All on board had perished.

Nicknames abounded amongst fishermen, to distinguish the many Rimmers, Wrights, Bonds and Leadbetters. In Fleetwood Mr T. Rimmer was known as Sparrow. His wife was doubly bereaved, having already lost a son at sea.

Early on the morning of 28 June 1887 a schooner, *Esther Ann*, timber-laden, bound from Wexford to Preston, was seen aground on Crusader Bank. The Blackpool lifeboat went out at 8.00 a.m. and reached the ship in an hour to hear the Captain shout, 'I cannot afford to pay. The bit of money I have is in this vessel and I'm afraid I'm going to lose her, but will you take my wife and her two children ashore?' He was informed that the RNLI made no charge and that the lifeboat would stand by. The *Esther Ann* began to float with the rising tide, bumping heavily, her pumps kept going, but the vessel managed to get over the bank and was soon on her way to Preston. In tow of the steamer *Bickerstaffe*, the lifeboat returned to Blackpool where a 5,000-strong crowd greeted her with cheers.

1 November 1887. Gales in the Mersey damaged the Tranmere stage, suspending traffic. Just two days later the first sod of Manchester Ship Canal was cut by Lord Egerton of Tatton. From 1887 to 1892 Fleetwood had two lifeboats, an indication of what a busy time this was, with cargo trade at its height. The boatbuilding trade was also doing very well, Messrs Gibson completing four new boats and two yachts in the first week of June 1887.

One of the great attractions at Fleetwood was watching between thirty and sixty smacks sail out with the tide, led by Skipper Philip Kay, a Manxman. Philip had a painting of the Rangoon of which he was very proud, and a bible inscribed 'Philip Kay, Admiral of the Fleet'. The auction of shares in *Dairymaid* and *Janes*

Collecting for Lifeboat Saturday, 1926, outside the old Lifeboat House, Fleetwood. Note, later the site changed.

Mary in August reflected brisk, high bidding. In September there were fears for the barque *Woodbine* which had left Fleetwood two months previously, thirty days being the average time for the journey. (The 1880s went down as notorious years for grinding vessels to pieces, years when 202,243 emigrants sailed from Liverpool for America or Canada.) On 12 January the *Frederick* of Fleetwood experienced mountainous seas whipped up by a hurricane, whilst on the 4th the *Daisy* went ashore on the rocks of Connister, off the Isle of Man. *John Turner-Turner*, after three hours of arduous effort, managed to retrieve the crew of five. The next tide warped the vessel off the rocks and knocked a large hole in her bottom.

January 1888. The barque *Albert William* was wrecked on the treacherous Horse Bank, which in those days was an island. For weeks the work of unloading its grain continued, Marshside fishermen carting to Southport Railway Station. One horse dropped dead going out to the wreck, and two horses were lost in the Bog Hole. It was a laborious job, sacks being brought on boats, with carts crossing at low tide, but the work of removing cargo was good business for the fishermen, who needed a source of income. Five thousand bags of grain were brought ashore. The *Albert William* was embedded in 9ft of sand, with her seams leaking and rudder washed away, but a steam pump relieved her of water and she was towed to New Brighton. Crowds walked over the sands every Saturday and were charged sixpence a head to be shown around, the money being given to the Marshside men who had lost their horses.

The January 1888 enquiry into the loss of *Athelston*, which sailed from Fleetwood, showed that spontaneous combustion had taken place in her cargo of coal.

28 March 1888. A terrible three-day storm drove the schooner *John W. Pearns* of Antwerp to shelter in the Isle of Man. She took up position near the Battery Pier, but when it became known that she had 800 cases of dynamite on board there was great anxiety and she was closely watched. At noon the cry went up that she was dragging her anchors, so off sped the *John Turner-Turner*, the coxswain telling the captain that the harbourmaster had given orders that he was to come off, as the lifeboat would not be allowed to go out again. Accordingly, captain and crew came ashore. The vessel did not drag her anchors but managed to ride the storm, leaving the bay safely a few days later.

7 December brought the glum news of a well-known schooner, *Princess Royal*, believed lost at sea. Built by Mr H. Warbrick, she was one of the Warbrick fleet associated with Captain Poole, who married Emily Warbrick.

7 October 1889. At 9.00 a.m. the Manx coast was struck by one of its worst gales. Through a powerful telescope a vessel could be seen driven on the rocks, with all its masts and gear carried overboard. Nothing but the stump of the mizzenmast remained. A steamer was seen to approach, remain two hours, but then continue southwards on her course. The distressed vessel lay broadside in the trough of the sea,

Persian with her beautifully raked masts and bottom.

Emily Warbrick, the famous top-sail schooner built on the beach at Fleetwood.

Launch of HMS *Princess Royal* at Vickers Works, Barrow, by HRH Princess Royal.

Parthis, of the Cunard Line, prior to sailing stormy seas from Liverpool in 1887, the year the Tancock foundered with a cargo of pitch pine from Novia Scotia.

and it was evident she was doomed. The lifeboat *John Monk* set off, having selected a crew from twenty volunteers to face five hours of awful battling, making tack after tack. They eventually arrived at what was now a complete wreck. All around floated spars, sails, ropes, and with not a moment to lose a struggle to save twenty-three souls began. First on the reeving line came the captain's wife, then the carpenter who had tied the captain's infant to his shoulders, and lastly the captain himself with a badly hurt youth who later died. Nevertheless, the triumph of getting back to shore with thirty-eight people alive was so tremendously overwhelming that both rescued and rescuers kissed the ground.

7

Landfall, Then Departure

The 1890s were productive of storms of such fury that even powerful steamships fell victim. On 24 January 1890 the *Thorne*, a magnificent vessel of 876 tons bound from Liverpool to Adelaide with general cargo and passengers, dropped anchor north of Connister to ride out the storm, but as it increased in fury, distress signals were sent up. The *Thomas Rose*, first on the scene, found the *Thorne* lying on the rocks to the north of Port Jack, and it appeared that in their terror the crew had taken to the boat, which was in imminent danger of swamping, being rendered unmanageable from the number of people who had crowded into her. But for the lifeboat's timely arrival, the seventeen would have been lost to the merciless sea. Johnny Kelly, the coxswain, showed the highest skill, not allowing the lifeboat to row towards the glimmer of light as it too could have landed on the rocks. He used a kedge anchor, and the men paid out the hawser till the ship's boat was reached. Five minutes longer would have been too late.

'Twenty-four men in twenty-four hours' was quoted in Fleetwood in November 1890 when yet again storms ravaged the Fylde coast. Amidst a scene of 'wild, weird grandeur' the lifeboat *Child of Hale* was launched because distress flares had been spotted. Coxswain Robert Wright directed her through blinding spray to the barque *Labora*, which had anchored in Lune Deeps. It took an hour to transfer the crew in desperately dangerous conditions with hurricane force winds blowing.

Under Captain Anton Skadberg the *Labora* had carried logwood roots all the way from Jamaica, but it proved to be the last voyage of a proud vessel. Man after man was pulled by lifeline through the relentless tempest, first a sick sailor utterly exhausted and lastly the captain with a clasp knife in his teeth, ready to hack at any entanglement of rigging. Only then could the lifeboat make for Fleetwood. But the work of rescue was not finished. At daylight the *New Brunswick* dragged her anchor, and, with masts cut away, was drifting helplessly. Robert Wright, coxswain, born 1832 and known far beyond Fleetwood for unflagging bravery, decided to launch the larger lifeboat *Edith*, using the tug boat to cut through the mountainous seas. During the five-mile run, waves crashed onto the lifeboat repeatedly and the crew of the *New Brunswick*, with ropes and masts dangling dangerously, had to be encouraged to leap.

The height of Fleetwood's timber and grain trade is revealed in this photograph of Wyre Dock. A 1,400-ton cargo of wheat had to be taken off the *Castlemaine* and reloaded under Board of Trade regulations on 15 October 1891. The iron-built schooner stuck on Bernard's Wharf and steam tugs *Fylde* and *Brock* failed to move her. The ship's plates split but the wheat was saved and the crew taken off.

So, amid the cheers of anxious crowds onshore, for the second time in twenty-four hours the lifeboat crew returned victorious, having saved as many men.

Examined on oath by the Receiver of Wreck, Hans Theodor Hansen, master of the *New Brunswick*, deposed as follows: 480 registered tonnage of the port of Bravig, Norway, owned by N.W. Coch, rigged as a barque, built of wood at Nova Scotia in the year 1864. Crew 11. Cargo of deals consigned to Blades of Lancaster. No passengers. In a very heavy sea blowing a hurricane from the north-west at 7 a.m., 5 November, her harbour cable parted, windlass carried away and bumping all the time, she finally grounded at Bernard's Wharf. The cause of wreck was finally recorded, 'stress of weather; a perfect hurricane blowing. In my opinion it could not have been avoided'.

Robert Wright, instrumental in his long career in saving 200 lives, was awarded a silver medal and pair of binoculars for gallantry. Other silver medallists of those years were Robert Gerrard, William Swarbrick, James Fogg, master of the smack *Osprey*, and George Wilkinson, one of the crew, the last two winning the medals for attempting to save the lives of the schooner *Jean Campbell* on 7 November 1890. James Abram and George Greenall died heroes, commemorated later by a monument in Euston Park, in sound and sight of the sea.

October 1892. A square-rigged, three-masted Norwegian barque, the *Sirene*, was driven by south-westerly gales to destruction on the hulking beside North Pier,

Blackpool. This was one occasion when the lifeboatmen did not have to put to sea. The crew were rescued by lowering ropes from the pier. Meanwhile, £500 worth of furs fell into the sea from a damaged shop on the pier. The same gale-force winds sent the Peel lifeboat to the rescue of a large vessel, *Indian Chief*, which was later in its career wrecked on the Goodwin Sands. On the Mersey, the Liverpool lifeboat went out to the *Maxwell*, which struck the bar. Twenty-nine men were rescued, but the lifeboat capsized. The crew hung on whilst the boat drifted to the Rock Channel, with two men missing and a third dying later from injuries. At high tide the cellars of the Starr Inn, South Shore, Blackpool, were flooded and the pumps in the bar 'produced sea water'. Waves played

Above and below: Lord Clive and *St Romans*, who also experienced heavy ice.

havoc with the sea fence hulking fronting Bailey's Hotel, and 'large stones were washed out as if they had been chips of wood'.

November 1893. The steamship *Odd* was wrecked in Morecambe Bay, and the three-masted schooner *Theda* of Caernarvon (139 tons), under Master Griffith Jones, from which eight were saved, was wrecked off Sunderland Point. On a voyage from Hamburg to Glasson Dock, carrying 260 tons of emiriate of potash, the *Theda*'s crew tried to get into the longboat but waves broke her in two. She was a wooden craft, built at Pwllheli in 1876, classed A1 at Lloyds. The mate, William Ellis, had been at sea thirty-four years and never before been shipwrecked.

Of all the ships that have foundered off the coast of Lancashire in memorable storms, one of the luckiest 'landings' was that of the *Huntcliff* in February 1894. Such was the wind force and flood of seas inland that rabbits and hares were seen running down the streets in Lytham, driven from their sandhills' home. Large advertising boards were uprooted and carried fields away; lead was ripped from roofs, but all such incidents paled into insignificance compared with the stranding of the steamship *Huntcliff* on the 12th. She was a cargo boat for which George Horsley & Sons of Hartlepool had paid £36,000 only two years before; an ocean tramp, 350ft in length, with a registered tonnage of 2,018 and engines equivalent to 1,700hp. Alongside her, the *Sirene*, stranded the previous year, would have looked comparatively paltry. The crew consisted of twenty-seven men, the Wilkes brothers of Middlesbrough being in charge of the magnificent engines. Five Arabs and a Zulu looked after the stoking, and, unknown to the captain, there were two stowaways on board.

Having made the run from Java to New York with sugar, the *Huntcliff* had come to Liverpool with a cargo of cotton from Charlestown. Bound for Cardiff, where she planned to load coal at Barry Dock for Aden, she left Liverpool at two o'clock on Sunday, carrying only water ballast and with a pilot on board. Absence of a cargo meant that a tremendous amount of hull was exposed to the violence of wind and waves, when at 5.00 p.m., just about four miles off Great Orme's Head, gales came roaring in. Despite her weight and size, the vessel was swung round with ease, for the rudder had no hold of the water, and when sails were set to keep her 'head on', the canvas was torn from the rigging like paper. Efforts to fix tarpaulins in the mizzen rigging were also futile. It was later said, 'If we had only had half a cargo we should have been able to steam against it'.

Captain Howell and Chief Officer Peterson decided to lie as near as possible to the coast of Llandudno, so let go anchor, but their plan failed. Worse still, the anchor could not be hauled up again and 120 fathoms of chain had finally to be sacrificed to the hungry sea. With the power of steam subdued, they could neither shelter nor put back into Liverpool. Broadside on, in the teeth of the gale, the *Huntcliff* rolled so fearfully, at the mercy of wind and ocean, that the crew had a hard time holding on. Their hands were sore with the effort. Terrified, the Arabs moved hither and thither about the companionways, and the stowaways, who had thought only of a cheap passage to Cardiff, dearly wished they had never come.

Between 5.00 on Sunday afternoon and 2.00 on Monday morning the *Huntcliff* was blown at the caprice of the elements until she bumped at St Annes. No stationary lights were seen during that appalling night. And so the hours dragged on until, no idea where they were, one wave lifted the mass of steel as though it were a plank of wood and tossed her into fifteen fathoms of water. On the crest of another huge wave she was seized again, carried a considerable distance and finally deposited, quite undamaged, on the sandy bottom of the beach not far from the Convalescent Home and only fifty yards from the sandhills. A better place for beaching could not have been chosen. Not one of her steel plates was buckled and there was many a joke made afterwards on the lines of 'Huntcliff is her name and she has lived up to it'.

News of the stranding of such a magnificent boat travelled fast. Crowds poured in from all over the district. Professional photographers, known in the nineteenth century as 'professors of the dark art', swarmed alongside amateurs. With difficulty black cloths were held over heads and heavy plate cameras; one moment intent on focussing, the next, cloth and camera were blown into the wind. At high tides clouds of spray broke over the decks and spectators venturing near received a thorough soaking.

Ice-cream stalls and fruit sellers set up, and by Wednesday the area of the vessel was described as a fairground. 800 people visited the scene, many brought in by railway, and so great was the crowd that few were allowed on board.

Meanwhile discussions went on as to how to move the *Huntcliff*. The underwriters sent Mr W. Horsley and Captain Young of Liverpool to size up the situation. As she was insured for £35,000, they were determined to float the *Huntcliff* at any cost. Should a channel be dug for her passage to the sea? The steam tug *Ranger* was expected to

A long-held belief on the Fylde was that the tide regulates death, the breath of life flickering as a wave flows to its height only to be extinguished as it retreats. It was said that old sailors 'crossed the bar' or 'went out with the tide'. Death was thought to be delayed by lying on a pillow stuffed with pigeon feathers and sea-sickness averted by hanging a bag of saffron in the stomach area. This 1893 photograph shows an ebbing tide in the channel off Knott End.

A photograph of the barque *Furu*, 22 December 1894, one of the many wrecked on Pilling Sands. One of the last hulks to go was the *Hamoaze* in the early 1970s, not without causing a great deal of trouble.

The stranding of the *Huntcliff* at St Annes-on-Sea, February 1894. Although she received a long battering at the mercy of the waves, she had a happy landing on the beach near the sand dunes, quite undamaged.

arrive with stores on board for this operation. Another plan was to build a ramp under her, lifting the tremendous weight by hydraulic jacks and to re-float on the 28ft tide expected on 20 February. This first method had already worked in the 1860s for a schooner which came ashore below the Central Pier area of Blackpool. On the 24th they managed it. Meanwhile the Arabs had been embroiled in a knife fight ashore, and another member of the crew had been found incapable on the genteel pavement of St Annes 'with a bottle of whiskey for a pillow'. So it was that both ship's crew and townspeople breathed a sigh of relief as the *Huntcliff* turned towards Liverpool.

The weird, mysterious tolling of a bell sounded doom-laden one snowy, stormy night in December 1894. It proved to be the Gassoon or buoy warning-bell broken loose from its moorings in Barrow Channel and driven across the bay, to be found later opposite Uncle Tom's Cabin. It was to prove a death knell to such ships as the *Abana*, built in 1874 at New Brunswick, Canada, registered tonnage 1,257. Even the sand froze on the beaches on Friday the 21st as the *Abana*, with 500 tons of ballast aboard and a crew of seventeen, buffeted across Liverpool Bay. The wind was freshening to gale force, following a lull, when suddenly a perfect hurricane struck. Canvas sails were torn to shreds, ripping off into the blackness; mizzen and fore topgallant sails went next. All they could do was run with the wind, blown backwards and forwards in the wild Irish Sea, which was excelling itself, driven by gusts reaching 100mph. All sails gone, the crew realised they were in grave danger. One man, already shipwrecked twice, anticipated a third baptism by sea.

Finally the *Abana*, after being tossed on Shell Wharf, floundered her way until she lay off Norbreck. The alarm was raised by Robert Hindle, landlord of the Cleveleys Hotel, who sent a messenger on horseback to alert the *Samuel Fletcher*, which had to be hauled overland by horses through Bispham village prior to launching. All the crew were taken off and were given beds at the old Red Lion Hotel. Mr Hindle was presented with the ship's bell and the captain's dog. The massive brass bell now adorns St Andrew's Church

The bell from the *Abana* wreck has recorded upon it, 'built in New Brunswick, Canada, 1874'. As Robert Hindle of the Cleveleys Hotel raised the alarm and got the lifeboat to rescue the crew of seventeen, he was presented with this bell, used to call parishoners to the institute. St Andrew's Church was built in 1910 and the bell, now hanging in the new north-west porch, built in 1976, is rung at every service for the interment of ashes at the Garden of Remembrance.

Above: A rough sea, from Central Pier, Blackpool.

Left: Three visitors in 1921 standing at the ribs of the *Abana* off Anchorsholme. The remains of this wreck still draw visitors like a magnet.

Christmas 1895 at Knott End when even the beaches and the sea froze. On 1 October a hurricane broke out on the Fylde coast. The *Geneva* and *Volunteer* were wrecked off the hulking at South Shore, Blackpool. The *Two Sisters* went down with all hands and other wrecks were scattered at Norbreck and Rossall.

Above and below: Figurehead of the *Abana*, wrecked off Anchorsholme, 22 December 1894. The shipwrecked mariners were taken to the Red Lion, Bipsham, where Mrs Hardman, the licensee, made them a Christmas dinner of plum pudding, beef and turkey. Captain Danielson and the crew were mainly Norwegian.

Crew of the *Abana* before wrecking, photographed on board. The ship's ribs are still to be seen in the sand not far from where *Riverdance* was wrecked.

porch. The plaque from her stern depicting a woman with long, flowing hair is fixed above a Lancashire plumber's workshop. The ribs of this sailing ship, something of a legend in Fylde, can still be seen. Also wrecked in that storm was the *Skulda*.

The hurricane caused havoc onshore. Fleetwood Rubber Works was blown down, windmills damaged, haystacks scattered, roofs lifted, oyster stalls at Blackpool overturned, one landing on the top of Central Station. In Morecambe Bay eight vessels were wrecked and nine Fleetwood fishermen died. A two-day blizzard lost three mothers their sons, and left nineteen children fatherless. Christmas was a time of deep sorrow, and the Fleetwood Disaster Fund was set up to ease the anguish. Smacks *Red Rose*, *Petrel*, *Surprise* and the *Mayflower* mourned Skippers Richard Wright and Robert Roskell, William Lynch, John Enright, James Ball and George Bond.

The Morecambe Bay lightship drifted from its moorings, thereby misguiding other vessels, and the wooden Norwegian barque *Furu*, built 1873, was wrecked on Pilling Sands. Registered in Finsberg, the *Furu* was 844 tons and had a crew of fourteen. She was left high and dry after braving a hurricane in which she lost her topsail, forestay and mizzen stay sail, until 5 a.m. when the crew walked ashore. Her back broken and keel torn away, she was a total wreck, sold later as salvage to local men. Captain Larsen made his report to the Receiver of Wrecks the next day.

Fishing smack *Petrel*, wrecked off the Gynn, Blackpool, December 1894.

A frozen Morecambe Bay.

Norwegian barque *Furu*, wrecked on Pilling Sands, September 1894.

When tempest rakes the Irish Sea, Fleetwood is inevitably a disaster zone, and as if it were not enough, in less than a year, in October 1895, another hurricane roared down. Two fishing boats, the *Genesta* and the *Volunteer*, were wrecked off South Shore, the sloop *Pearl* wrecked on a groyne near Rossall, and the *Two Sisters* went down like a stone with all hands in the early morning of 2 October. Five fishing boats were missing from Fleetwood, leaving eight widows and thirty-two children under fourteen fatherless. An appeal was made, not only to residents and visitors of Blackpool, Lytham, Fleetwood and St Annes, but throughout the country. The loss of the barque *Highland Home* (November 1895) also struck hardest at Fleetwood. Widows received from the fund 5*s* per week for eight years, though *Highland Home* widows got only 4*s* for a similar period. Each child had 2*s* a week until they reached the age of fourteen. One Fleetwood sailor, perceiving what he called 'cobwebs floating across the moon', refused to sail on 2 October 1895, viewing it as a warning of disastrous weather, but the majority went because it was their living, and there were many mouths to feed.

The terrific north-west gale of Tuesday and Wednesday, 1 and 2 October 1895, strewed the Fylde coast with wrecks, but destruction came so suddenly that the lifeboats could render no assistance. At about six o'clock on the Wednesday the *Daisy*

The *Pearl*, wrecked at Norbreck, October 1895.

of Fleetwood was seen tearing helplessly before the gale. As the smack flew past North Pier jetty, Blackpool, a sailor was seen to climb the mast only to disappear in an instant as the small craft was clawed into the raging sea. Another wreck was seen on Salthouse Bank, as the tide went down, with not a soul on board. This was all that remained of the *Edith* of Morecambe. Beaches from Fleetwood to Lytham were littered with spars, torn sails and bodies. Indeed, some of the drowned fishermen were not found for months.

16 June 1897 proved, as in many a previous summer, that the ferocity of its storm can be no whit less than those of deepest winter. (Such a one was that of June 1833.) Admiral Nelson's old flagship, The *Foudroyant*, was on show at Blackpool after restoration and refitting at a cost of £20,000 by Mr G.W. Cobb, who could not bear to see the grand old warrior towed off to Germany. After a short spell at Southport, the most famous surviving ship of the British Navy, which had carried the flag of Lord Nelson as commander-in-chief of the Mediterranean, was taken to Blackpool. The captain was warned that he could be in difficulties if the wind rose, but William John Robins was quite confident and paid no heed. The *Foudroyant*, carrying sixty cannons in three tiers, anchored

Foudroyant timbers were made into souvenirs: walking sticks, jewel boxes, tables. Some of the metal was made into medallions depicting the ship with details of events stamped on the obverse.

The *Foudroyant*. The spectacular wrecking off Blackpool of one of the most famous ships of all time, Lord Nelson's flagship.

The *Foudroyant*, wrecked in 1897, a victim of the Irish Sea's fury.

FOUDROYANT

between Central and North Piers. A gale began early in the morning of Wednesday 16 June 1897. The *Foudroyant* broke from her moorings, was carried helplessly by the great force of the storm, and grounded on the shore near the North Pier. From the Wellington Hotel, Blackpool, Wheatley Cobb wrote to his mother at Caldicott Castle:

> We went back to the ship yesterday and her condition was horrifying. The huge old timbers are ripped in every direction, every internal fitting and bulk head swept away and the decks rent to pieces, The violence with which she bumped is shown by the lower deck guns having ploughed grooves three feet deep through the solid oak sides ... for six hours we were cold and hungry and drenched, the ship striking heavily every minute or two and going to pieces. The upper masts were bending like whips and the first to go was the fore t'gallant. If we had jumped overboard, no one could have lived two minutes in the sea. I never saw any waves half so big as they where, all rough and broken floods of water swept through the shattered door of the Admiral's cabin ... then a shout went up that the lifeboat had put out. We got in and were landed into a crowd of several thousands.

It was not until 1.50 p.m.that the lifeboat *Samuel Fletcher* had been able to rescue the crew of the *Foudroyant*, and if that account does not prove the furious capability of the Irish Sea then nothing will. Blackpool's lively and enterprising Advertising Manager, Mr C. Nadin, telegraphed the news all over the country, bringing trainloads of crowds to pick up souvenirs, wood, bolts and scraps of copper. Mr Cobb employed a salvage company from Glasgow, striking the arrangement that if they failed to re-float her they could have the ship for £10 and be paid nothing. Guns and figurehead were recovered, the latter being preserved at Caldicott Castle, but an attempt to float the vessel failed. The remains were sold and made into articles for tourists. Thus a great and magnificent ship met its end at the height of storm and tempest. Perhaps it was a better end than the original one decreed by the ruthless decision of the Admiralty: 'sold out of service to a Plymouth ship breaker for £2,000'.

But the *Foudroyant* had still not had the last word. Two vessels were wrecked trying to salvage her timbers, and at the end of November another raging sea smashed what remained of her to bits, dismembering every oak plank and beam. The same storm got the steamship *Larnica* into difficulty. Twenty were rescued by Fleetwood lifeboat.

The great 'Jubilee' gale blew for three days during which time five wrecks were claimed off Fleetwood. A Scottish schooner, *Countess of Selkirk*, built in 1861 at Charlestown, came ashore at Norbreck. Under the command of Master William McQuie, she was carrying fifty tons of timber, shipped by Hogg & Co., when the squall took jib and foresail and damaged her rudder. Coxswain Leadbetter, directing the lifeboat, saved twenty-three from the barque *Louisa*, the barque *Svallen* of Frederickstad and the steamship *Zillah*. The soldiers under canvas had their beds, bedding and tents blown in all directions by the sportive winds.

This unknown wreck, probably from Liverpool, is seen lying off Formby.

Thought to be a shipwreck at Formby about 1898. The turnout of curious spectators sometimes hampered the work of salvage. Deliberate wreckers became known as 'people without fear of God'.

October 1898. A deposition made by William Marshall, master of the *Minnie*, registered at Liverpool, 63 tons, a wooden ketch built 1875 at Rhyl, showed that she was carrying a cargo of corn for Parkinson & Tomlinson, millers of Poulton-le-Fylde. She sailed from Liverpool on 20 October from Alexandra Dock with her regulation lights in good order, burning brightly, about 9ft from the deck, also with a white stern light hanging outside the bulwarks.

On Thursday 20 October, at 11.40 p.m., on a half-flood tide, very dark, nearly opposite Knott End Spit Gas Buoy, under jib, staysail, mainsail and mizzen, with the master at the helm, she was hit by the *Duke of Cornwall*. The crew of the *Minnie* had to get on board the *Duke of Cornwall* by means of lines thrown to them. 'Cause of casualty was the Duke of Cornwall altering her course when she showed her red light: might have been avoided if that vessel had continued her course and kept under the stern of deponent's vessel'.

April 1898. The steam trawler *Diana of Grimsby* got into difficulties, as did the barque *Margarethe* in May. In both cases the Fleetwood lifeboat assisted, being towed to the wrecks by the steam tug *Lune*. The *Margarethe* was not insured.

A wreck off the Skerries in March, when the vessel broke up, cast its cargo on stormy waters which washed up large quantities of apples even as far away as Rossall. They were collected, sold on Fleetwood market and pronounced 'tip-top'. Several carcases of cattle from the same wreck were also tossed onto northern shores. Southport had its share of casualties in the 1890s, one of interest being the schooner *Gelion* of Norway, wrecked on Spencer's Bank on 8 September 1891. The crew were rescued by the pleasure steamer *Bickerstaffe* whose captain received the Board of Trade silver medal.

Both the romance and drama of the sea are brought out in two incidents from the final year of the nineteenth century. A remarkable story, beginning in 1898, concerns the Fylde and its link with the oceans of the world. The ship *Samoena*, having set sail for Oregon, found itself five months later in dire straits. A member of the crew placed the following message in a bottle which he sealed and cast overboard: '130 days out and no provisions on board. Crew on half whacks, living on cargo of wheat and don't expect to reach port ever. If this is picked up send word to E.S. Fardon, 11 Agnew Street, Lytham, Lancashire, England'. The bottle was picked up at Parrot Bay, West Indies, at Christmas 1899, and the message was sent on to Lytham. In the meantime the sailor's friends had heard from him, as he had reached port alive. Commander Captain Simpson of the White Star Line made it a custom to throw well-stoppered bottles bearing messages overboard in all parts of the world. By 1911 he had received 1,000 back.

The second incident concerns a Fleetwood-bound vessel, the *Broughton*, which in 1899 hit a cyclone. The captain died: the officers and men were sick and close to death from starvation, yet eventually they did manage to dock at Fleetwood.

These years saw most of the great lifeboat rescues. They involved seemingly insurmountable difficulties – establishing communications in howling gales, constant danger from wrecks suddenly listing, loose flapping masts and rigging, flying spars, enveloping canvas, strong sudden currents, coping with injured, shocked passengers and sailors reduced to states of terror. There are tales of lifeboats struggling through sand and snow drifts. They never gave up when there was a chance to save lives, unless the pandemonium of wind and sea raging like mad made it impossible to approach, and on such occasions the feelings of these gallant men may well be imagined, for they staked all without a thought for their own safety.

A depiction of a sailing ship in the brickwork of the Conservative Club in Poulton-le-Fylde, a reminder of bygone days. This building was originally the Ship Inn.

The *City of Liverpool* looks peaceful enough moored at Glasson Dock in the early years of the twentieth century, but she had experience of the damaging power of heavy seas.

Crossfields' Boat builders' Arnside old port.

Viaduct at Arnside with a train in the centre, *c.* 1988.

8

SEAGULLS FLY HIGH

One of many quaint beliefs held by old sailors was that the higher flew the seagulls, the greater and more sudden would be the storm, and one wonders how true this is. The boatyard of Crossfields, Arnside, like that of Armours of Fleetwood, made some well-known vessels, yachts and prawners, in its time, and one fine yacht was delivered to Mr John Jackson on 8 December 1900. An experienced ferryman in the area, Mr Jackson intended to race Cock o' the North in the many popular regattas then organised in the Bay. Leaving Arnside on a clear day, with alarming suddenness a gale bore down upon him, ripping the mainsail. Two anchors were dropped but both broke clear as the gale increased in force, leaving the crew with nothing for it but to jump overboard, struggling ashore as best they could whilst there was yet time. Helplessly, they watched the new vessel, never to be seen again, battered and driven off to sea by hurricane-whipping waves.

On 21 December 1900 the crew of the Lytham lifeboat boarded a derelict, drifting, four-masted barque, the *Glasgow*. In what Mr C.A. Myers, honorary secretary of the RNLI considered one of the most exciting and interesting of salvage operations in the Ribble Estuary, the lifeboat crew received £200 each and all who helped were rewarded. At an enquiry on 31 July 1901 it was decided that the SS *Agamemnon* of Liverpool must take full responsibility for sinking the Fleetwood schooner *Saxon Maid* as the former had been travelling far too fast for foggy conditions.

A sale of shipwrecked goods was held in Blackpool on 15 July 1902, thousands of pounds worth of articles and materials salvaged from SS *Mimidia* and SS *Java*. For variety alone the list is worth perusing. T. Bannister's Bazaar offered 40,000 fine, lawn handkerchiefs for 10½*d* a dozen, 26,000 pieces of cloth (mulls, velvets, jaconettes, meltons, pure silks, calicoes), hand-woven curtains, French and Indian cretonnes, scarves, Chinese and Indian velvet squares, fringes, 30,000 yards of red, white and blue bunting (1¾*d* a yard), Dresden China, Silurian notepaper, and the most bizarre item of all, which reads like a line from an Edward Lear poem: 15,000 ping-pong sets at 5½*d* each.

Once into the twentieth century, the greater use of steam and new types of engines enabled vessels to weather out most bad storms. Wrecks were fewer with longer intervals between. A rough calculation for Southport was put at 300 wrecks

The lighter *Rossall*, which was used to take off cargo from ships that ran into trouble, driven onto sandbanks during storms.

The three-masted *Valkyrien* (right), 1902, and others positioned on the gridiron at Fleetwood Docks, ready for repairs. (Courtesy of the late Mr Blackledge)

between 1745 and 1946, with 1,100 lives saved. Receding tides at Southport were causing people to think it was becoming an inland town, but Rossall and Fleetwood, who had always borne the brunt, still had a fair number of incidents to report.

In the early years of the twentieth century, as if to prove itself still master, a tidal wave engulfed the Arnside-Heversham area, sweeping away an artificial tide barrier, the Lugg, and inspiring a minor classic: Constance Holme's *The Lonely Plough*. The rushing tidal bore covered the north end of Morecambe Bay, Aldingham and Leighton Moss, a reminder of the great tidal storm during the reign of Edward I, which washed away the sixteenth-century church, then at the centre of the village.

Even more devastating was to be the 1927 flood which engulfed an entire modern town, Fleetwood, with loss of life. A Fleetwood fishing smack was wrecked off Ramsey, Isle of Man, with one seaman drowned in February 1902. On 9 March 1903 the fishing smack *Montpelier* came ashore on the Horse Bank (two crew and two passengers being saved by lifeboat). The Fleetwood schooner *Lancashire Lass* was wrecked off the Scottish coast, drowning one of the crew. Gales persisted into March when 'a terrible storm' ravaged the *Duke of York*, whose voyagers during the crossing were described as 'very scared – driven to distraction' as 50ft-high waves powered by a 90mph wind pounded the steamer. Captain Jackson, master of the *City of Belfast*, said it was one of the Irish Sea's best performances; 'as wild as in 1894' when Commodore John Cook of the *Duke of York* reported a cyclone at sea.

On 6 October 1903 two sandbarges of 300 tons belonging to Preston Corporation dragged anchors and drifted before the gale. One crashed through Lytham Pier and the other collided with the Pavilion's ironwork. The anchor stuck fast so that one barge was held with its stern wedged beneath the building. Messrs D. Hedges & Son of Lytham took a very good photograph.

It was on Monday 2 March 1903 that the wooden three-masted schooner *Vanadis* came to grief in Half Moon Bay, the marshland next to where Heysham Harbour was built. A Russian vessel under Captain J. Anderson, she was completed in 1874 at Jacobstad (length 185ft, breadth 35.1ft, gross tonnage 1,702), her owner being V. Sundmau.

Storm-blown into the bay, she went aground with a cargo of timber and became dismasted. As attempts to re-float her were considered hopeless, the vessel was declared a total wreck, the cargo dragged from the stern opening, loaded onto horse-drawn carts and sold to the highest bidder. With the hull stripped of scrap metal, weather and time took their toll and, like the *Abana*, all that now remain are the ribs of the keel, visible according to shift of tides.

The ship's figurehead was once on view in Heysham Head Leisure Park, but it has since vanished from the scene. Not far from the *Vanadis* also lie the remains of the *Pudyona*, which supplied a flagstaff from its wreck timbers for Morecambe Promenade and which gave her name to a stretch known ever afterwards as Pudyona Sands.

Some of the crew of the TSS *Duke of York*, launched 23 February 1894. Mrs McCaffrey is in hat and apron, seated with Mr Piper; Mr Cowell; A. Cardon (pantry boy); and Mr Wilks (steward). A terrible storm with 50ft waves struck the vessel in March 1903. She was a Lancashire and Yorkshire Railway Co. ship.

Lytham Docks in 1950.

The village of Bare, near Heysham where the *Venadis* came to grief.

Liv, rigged as a barque, built in 1854 and rebuilt in 1880, became a casualty on 16 October 1903. A Norwegian vessel of 246 tons owned by H. Cornelinsen of Larvig, she had a crew of seven and sailed from Douglas on 14 October bound for Norway. A strong south-south-east breeze turned into a crippling gale… 'The vessel met with baffling winds and thick weather'. Lying at anchor off Wyre Light, her chain broke and she was driven onto Pilling Sands. The lifeboat *Maude Pickup* rescued and landed the crew at Fleetwood around 7.45 p.m.

Some Lancashire vessels were involved in collisions in 1904. The trawler *Young Walker*, owned by Councillor R. Westby, was wrecked off Orme's Head, the crew being rescued by the steamer *Innsfallen*. The *Duke of Gordon* and *Carrick* sank in a collision off the Firth of Clyde, Captain Leadbetter of Fleetwood going down with his ship, the *Carrick*. Two members of the crew of the Fleetwood trawler *Kitty* were drowned in Tobermory Harbour in November 1905. During March that year work on removing five wrecks from Pilling Sands proceeded well, leaving only the remains of *Liv* and *Furu*.

Wrecks in this area served as targets for firing practice in later years. Indeed, a determined attempt was made to blow them up because they were a danger to shipping, but the shocks and reverberations resulted in complaints from the residents. One of Moody & Kelly's trawlers, the *Crown*, was wrecked in 1906, a stormy year with the usual November gales. The steam trawler *Belmont* was driven onto Pilling Sands near Knott End slipway. As gales struck again, workmen lightening her bunker of coal were in danger and at noon the *Maude Pickup* lifeboat was launched to rescue them.

The Slipway, December 1917. The boat is the *City of Selby* FD8.

The wooden barque *Clara*, 430 tons, built in 1857 at Miramichi, directed by Olaf Petterson of Norway, was wrecked with her cargo of 56 tons of wooden deals which were being shipped to Preston in December 1906. The *Clara* had tried hard to get a pilot, asked assistance of a tug about one mile south of Nelson buoy, but was eventually forced to proceed unaided. (Although the pilot cutter was flying the flag, no pilot was on board.) Freshening heavy squalls drove the barque on, to strike bottom with her keel at midnight. Her main topmast came down under the continual bumping and she could not get into deep water. At daybreak, one mile from Rossall Landmark, her stern post broken, she was making water fast. There was no sign of the crew from shore where the signal gun to man the lifeboat had brought the population flocking in thousands to get a good view of the barque from the promenade. Things looked ominous when just after eight o'clock the lifeboat set off in charge of Coxswain Leadbetter. The tug *Fylde* had soon to assist, because halfway up the channel it was obvious that the crew could make no progress against the boisterous tide. Captain Petterson explained later that they were about to capsize as the main topmast smashed the rigging, sails blew away and a portion of the rudder went, so they took to the boat and were blown helplessly adrift on the dangerous, extensive sands. Drenched, buffeted and hungry, the crew of various nationalities had had a wild adventure and were thankful to be landed at Fleetwood. It was the twenty-fifth journey *Clara* had made to Preston, hitherto without mishap.

On a similar fierce, gusty day, that trusty warrior, well-named *Old Hunter*, was wrecked on Shell Wharf on 20 February 1906 with a cargo of coal bound for Mevagissey. Schooner *Maggie Kelso* also got into difficulties at 'the Neckings'. With great skill *Maude Pickup* took the exhausted crew of four from *Old Hunter*, and then proceeded to the *Maggie Kelso*. Left high and dry, the next day crowds went out to look at the wreck. A press photographer, in order to keep his equipment dry, was carried out on the back of a burly fisherman. Crews described the wind at the time of the wrecking as akin to a flaying machine, with the *Old Hunter* trembling like a pack of cards about to collapse at any moment. The wooden ship took a thunderous beating from the flapping canvas which made the masts buckle and leap.

Joseph Johnson, aged twenty-eight, a sign writer of Fleetwood, went as a passenger on the Lancashire in 1907 and lost his camera, bicycle and his entire holiday luggage. The SS *Lancashire*, built at Montrose, a two-masted steamer of 240 tons, owned by Fisher & Tindell of Liverpool, foundered near Bootle. She was conveying a cargo of purple ore from Widnes to Workington when she sprang a leak off Morecambe,

Clara.

Shipwrecked sailors landed at Fleetwood from the wreck of the *Old Hunter*, 1906.

The *Old Hunter* was a wooden schooner, copper fastened with timbers salted except beams, 95 gross tons, 81ft in length, 21ft breadth, 10ft depth, built at Berwick by Gowan in 1877, owners J. Fisher & Sons.

but proceeded hopefully to St Bees Head, where it was decided to make for Barrow. Matters abruptly worsened, forcing crew and passenger to take to the ship's boat. The cook had nothing on except his shirt; the others were only partly dressed.

It was a dark and cold night but thus they remained, miserably huddled on the shore, not daring to venture on the sandhills, until daylight when Strawberry Cottage, the holiday home of Dr Fitzgerald of Accrington, was seen nearby. At first he was dubious of their story, but the sight of the Lancashire was proof, whereupon he made them welcome, discovering in his well-meaning efforts to give stimulants that six of the woe-begone men were tee-total.

The Royal Albert Hall, Silecroft, later housed the crew and Mr Johnson, who were none the worse for their adventure, but the sad state of the *Lancashire*, flung onto her side, fittings cast upon the beach, was self-evident to the salvage steamer *Plover* of Liverpool, which arrived on the scene by Sunday afternoon with a representative of the owners.

December 1907 brought news to Fleetwood that the steam trawler *Rosedale* had been wrecked at Londonderry. On 28 December 1908 the *Albany* went on the rocks at Mull of Kintyre, and December 1909 experienced one of the classic gales. From three until five o'clock. the gale registered on the anemometer of the Mount as 93.33mph. The *Seagull*, a trawler tied up at Barrow, broke from its moorings and smashed. Amongst a plethora of incident, James Dewhurst, engine driver, was blown over by the wind and knocked unconscious. This wild storm also finished the plucky little steamer *Ellen Vannin*, affectionately known to Manx sailors as 'Lil'l Daisy'. Her name prior to 1883 was *Mona's Isle*, a

Aboard a steam trawler, 1915.

paddle steamer of 339 tons built in 1860 by Tod & Macgregor of Glasgow, then converted in 1883 to a twin-screw steamer, re-boilered and fitted with a new engine.

On 3 December 1909 the *Ellen Vannin* left Ramsey for Liverpool at 1.13 a.m. with fourteen passengers, mail and cargo. A severe north-west gale developed. At 6.45 a.m. she foundered between the Bar and No.1 Buoy, at the entrance to the Mersey. The storm was acknowledged to be one of the worst ever experienced. Although the ship was seaworthy, the crew good, it was the power of the sea that overcame within minutes, 24ft-high waves filled up and sank her with the loss of thirty-three lives.

'One of the most remarkable and one of the most profitable vessels owned by the company, she could always be relied upon for emergency service', said the speaker of the Manx House of Keys, Mr A. Moore, who was later to write a history of Isle of Man boats. £1,000 was given by the Steam Packet Co. and all the towns on the Fylde coast were invited to augment the relief fund ('the members of the crew alone have left 72 children dependent on them'). Divers reported that the *Ellen Vannin*'s plates were cut through by the violent impact of a 70mph gale meeting a contrary tide.

In January 1910 a collision occurred in the River Lune between the *Duke of Cornwall* and the smack *Elizabeth Ann*, in which the latter sank. A seaman had to use his thumb as a temporary plug in this incident.

Also in January 1910 the trawler *City of Bristol* was wrecked off the Antrim coast in the first week of the year. In August a gale caused the *Viking* to have a very bad crossing. *Kilburn* of Glasgow was wrecked in Morecambe Bay and sent flares for the lifeboat to be called. Normally the *Viking*, a crack ship of the Isle of Man Steam Packet Co., built in 1905 by Armstrong-Whitworth, with her triple screws, powered by three steam turbines, managed the crossing to Fleetwood in well under three hours, her record being two hours and twenty-two minutes on 25 May 1900. The two-masted steamer *Hebe* from Bergen, 3,500 tons, came ashore on the Horse Bank on 11 December 1911. The crew of twenty-one were saved, but not the vessel. Ship's master, Captain Robinson, had a cargo of wood pulp to take to Preston. For weeks afterwards Lytham children had fun picking up bits to convey home for burning. The *Rosaleen*, also off Lytham, became a total loss, but her crew of twenty-one were saved. It was reported on 9 January 1912 that the *Glenesk*, a Norwegian barque of 2,500 tons on a voyage from Middlesbrough to Fremantle with pig iron, had been seen in difficulties on New Year's Day. Attempts to take the barque in tow were foiled three times by the hawser breaking. Steam trawler *Rosetta* of the Rossall Steam Fishing Co. gave help and eventually landed the *Glenesk*, whose crew had suffered great privation, at Morville, after towing her 100 miles.

The Captain of the barque told the skipper of the *Rosetta* that on Christmas Day they had met the full force of a gale which carried away their foremast, main halyard and all the rigging, since when they had been drifting helplessly. The crew of the *Rosetta* received £825 for handling the disabled barque in what was a good year for fishermen in salvage work. The crew of the *Wrenthorpe* was awarded £550 for towing a cassion to Hoylake. Gallantry awards for saving life at sea were numerous: Messrs R. Robson, J.R. Scott and J. Cowell received silver medals, R. Leadbetter a pair of binoculars, W. Scott the Royal Humane Society's medal and R.S. Buxton the Board of Trade gallantry award. A coal strike caused hardship but kept trawlers out of danger because they could not put to sea.

On 20 November 1914 the *Doris*, known as 'Little Doris', foundered with three men drowned. On 14 December 1914 the oil tanker *Vedra*, 4057 tons, ran aground west of Walney Island. Loaded with benzene, travelling to Barrow from Texas with a crew of thirty-six, this involved a dangerous rescue mission. The Barrow and Fleetwood lifeboats had put out when suddenly there was a huge explosion followed by the sight of the *Vedra* and the sea aflame, making it impossible to get near. The cries of the injured and dying were audible to the lifeboat crews witnessing this inferno which burned for days. Buildings far away were rocked by the explosion. Of the three men who jumped into the sea, there were only two survivors as one died in hospital from burns. Southport lost a fishing smack in 1914, driven on Spencer's Bank, two of the crew being saved but the vessel becoming a total loss.

On 14 February 1915 the *Abeokuta*, built 1901 (Elder Dempster, R. Duncan & Co., 1817 tons, 280.2ft by 40ft by 18.2ft, with triple expansion engines), a British steamer

The crack ship of the line, the *Viking*, showing an Irish mail boat in the distance. The *Viking*'s stormiest crossing was in 1910, around the time of this photograph.

A Liverpool ship-owner.

sailing from Liverpool to West Africa with general cargo, was wrecked. The *Henry J. Smith*, a four-masted vessel from New York, voyaging between Liverpool and Cardiff, was lost in 1916 because the tow rope broke away from the tug in charge, the vessel drifting onto Freshfield Sands. Four lifeboats went to assist her. The Ulverston-built *Coniston* was lost off Millom in 1917.

13 April 1917 was an unlucky day for the *Francis Peel*, a Southport fishing smack, as she struck the wreck of the *Hebe* and sank within five minutes. The crew were hauled on board another smack. Also in April 1917 the steamer *Zelandia* stuck on the Horse Bank with a cargo of sheep. As the tide fell, her crew walked ashore. It was possible to re-float the *Zelandia* and return her to Liverpool.

The rescue of the Pittan's crew is still remembered in Fleetwood. A Russian barquentine, built of wood in 1898, Kari Behrsin was master carrying a cargo of pitch bound for Cadiz, Spain. At dead low water a north-west gale sprang up with heavy hail showers. An anchor was dropped but the cable parted and the barquentine grounded with heavy seas breaking aboard, all this being seen by the look-out on Wyre Light who signalled for the tug boat *Cleveleys* to proceed from harbour. It was the lifeboat, however, that rescued the crew. The vessel became a total loss (due entirely to heavy seas and gale) estimated by the master at £5,000 sterling. Sailing instructions were also lost with the vessel, which was not insured.

A steamer, *Chrysopolis*, heading from Genoa to Liverpool with a cargo of copper ore, struck on Spencer Bank off Southport on 1 February 1918, breaking her back and becoming a complete loss. Happily, the lifeboat rescued forty-two of her crew. Also in 1918 the schooner *Sunbeam*, from Holyhead to Preston carrying china clay, was wrecked, but her crew were saved by the lifeboat.

On 23 June 1919 the three-masted schooner *Herbert Black*, owned by the Atlantic Maritime Co., Boston, 662 tons, was wrecked off Marshside while taking a cargo of deals to Preston. The Lytham lifeboat took off the crew and Captain Glynn. When the steam trawler *Feugh* ran ashore at Bispham on 8 June 1923 her cargo of fish was taken by horse and cart and speedily galloped to Fleetwood market for sale. Cargo trade off the coasts declined with the nineteenth century during which vessels had come from ports all over the world, its place being taken by the fishing industry. Thus accounts of wrecked trawlers become a feature of the history of the seas.

There were exciting scenes on Blackpool Promenade when the *Ophir* was seen to be in distress. The exploding of two maroons, denoting a launching, had the effect of turning thousands of persons towards the Front. Fortunately by 1923 a wreck was becoming a rare event and none wanted to miss an unfolding real-life drama. The coasting steamer *Ophir*, 171 registered tonnage, belonging to the Zillah Shipping Co., Liverpool, was in the charge of Skipper John Sullivan and a crew of seven, carrying 480 tons of gravel to Liverpool. By two o'clock it could be seen that the vessel had a

Commandant Bultinck, 2 October 1929, wrecked off Rossall.

'Couch' Wright in either *Judy* or *Charlotte* (prawner). He saved the men of *Commandant Bultinck*.

distinct list to port, with heavy seas breaking, and that she was making every effort to reach Blackpool.

Forming a long, dark thread along the shoreline, people scurried to get as close as possible. Meanwhile, as news spread, thousands more joined the throng. By now the skipper of the *Ophir* had his boat opposite the Victoria Hotel and dropped two anchors. Captain and crew were reluctant to leave. They asked for a Lloyds agent and felt confident that if twenty men could help them (the cargo of gravel had shifted) they could right the boat. The gang arrived by tram with picks and shovels at eight o'clock, but waited until the morning to commence work. Meanwhile it was thought safer to get the crew ashore, but the lifeboat had to go three times to persuade them. The Shipwrecked Mariners Society took the crew in hand, providing clothes, steaming-hot tea and hefty beef and ham sandwiches. Captain Sullivan was unabashed. 'I like coming to Blackpool', he said, 'but I prefer to come in a charabanc and not like I did to day'. The *Ophir* was re-floated on 30 January.

One of the last dramatic sea adventures of the twentieth century was off Rossall where the *W.K. Chapman* had been wrecked on 28 September 1875, leaving the beach between the Landmark and Rossall School strewn with wreckage which included the ship's bell. The Belgian steam trawler *Commandant Bultinck*, wrecked on 2 October 1929, screamed her peril at midnight by the incessant sounding of her siren. Rossall schoolmasters and boys, wearing coats over their pyjamas, formed a human chain with others who had assembled on shore. In a storm of incredible fury, causing tremendous seas to run, some of her crew clung to the mast while others huddled in the wheelhouse. Hail, rain, thunder and lightning, with a cruel gale of 60mph, formed a classic backdrop. The black storm clouds, rent by lightning, threw up in high relief the tilting bulk of the *Commandant Bultinck* with the heavy waves continuously sluicing her deck. As soon as the tide began to recede the crew of twelve made suicidal leaps. Straight away three were lost, but others reached the shore via ropes and the human chain. Heedless of their own safety, people dashed into the waves to drag the exhausted, terrified men ashore. 'Couch' Wright of Fleetwood has admitted only in recent years that he was one of the unsung heroes of that night, going back into the sea several times. The Belgians were to come again to Fleetwood, sailing from Ostend on Tuesday 21 May 1946, fleeing the German invasion. One such family was the Van Beirs, who never forgot Fleetwood's hospitality and who, until the death of Mr Van Beirs, returned year after year.

As usual the crew were cared for at the Royal National Mission for Deep Sea Fishermen, which had grown from a branch of the British and Foreign Bible Society. In the days of sail, Mr W.H. Dickenson, missionary, learned Norwegian as so many of that nationality came to Bethel. Services were also held on board ship. In 1894 the Sailors' Rest was built 'on the site occupied by Mr Gibson, ship-

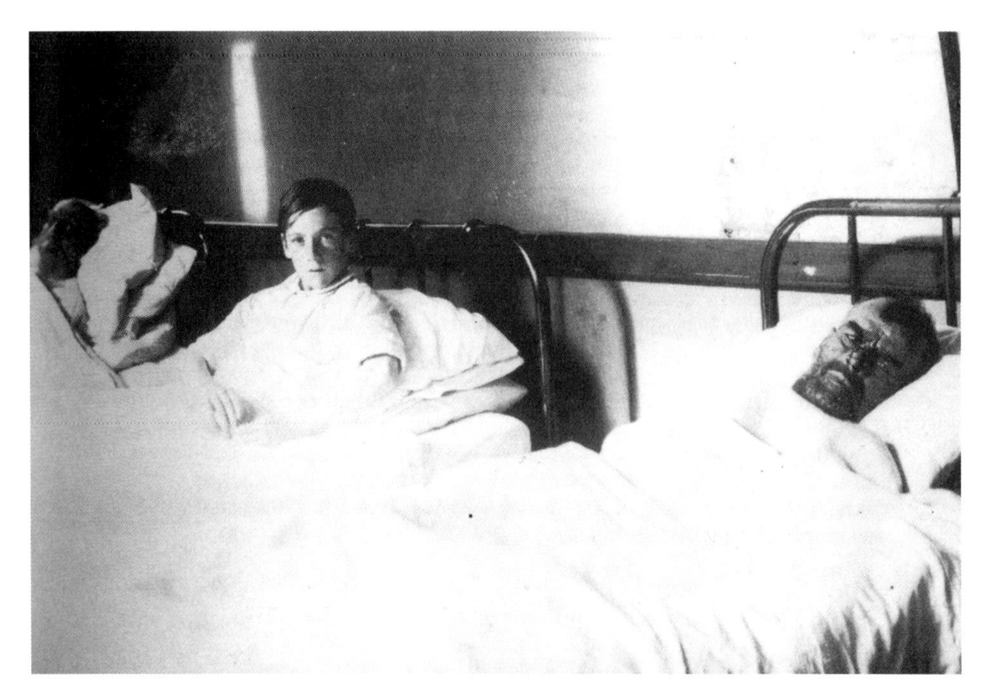

'50 Dead as Gale Sweeps Country. Sea Devastates a Town. Darkness, No Work and 1,223 Houses Flooded'. Such were October 1927 headlines. Thirteen fishermen died, caught in the storm of the Irish Sea. The photograph shows survivors of the 1927 Great Flood, recovering in the Fleetwood Cottage Hospital. Five people were drowned, an amazingly low number considering the engulfment that caused furniture to bump into ceilings. People stepped from bedroom windows into rescue boats. Promenades on the Fylde coast were torn to pieces by the gale's fury. 'The worst storm in the history of Fylde', resulted in an album of commemorative photographs recording the devastation.

builder', the gift of benefactress Mrs Fielden of Todmorden, and opened by Charles W. Macara. Perhaps the words of the mate of the schooner *Theda* in 1893 bore fruit: 'We landed at Fleetwood exhausted, strangers in a strange place, and knew not where to go and what to do.'

9

Wrecks for Sale

As sailing vessels became rare and steamers took over in the shipping lanes, losses at sea dropped, although storms still raged with awesome regularity in the Irish Sea areas. Indeed, although modern technology has reduced the incidence of wrecks, so long as man trusts himself to the oceans the story of founderings and complete disappearances will go on. Once into the twentieth century, the passing of the beautiful white-winged sailing ships brought with it a nostalgic desire to retain this legacy of memories. There was a time when to sweeten the note of a ship's bell, gold and silver were thrown into the casting crucible. Like the figurehead, the bell was preserved beyond the life of the ship and not usually re-engraved as that would bring bad luck. For more luck keels had to be 'well and truly laid', the favoured woods being ash or dogwood, abhorred by witches. Gold coins were included in the keel-splicing, the place being known only to the ship's owner and the master boat builder. Such enduring mystique clung; captains hated to lose a figurehead, even chippings from them were prized to the point of worship, yet the carver's fee was often paltry. The figurehead of the Fleetwood pilot boat *Falcon*, carved by L. Fitzimmons, was £3. Such work went into the making and maintaining of sea-going vessels, wrecked and lying on the sea-bed, whose history represented an appalling catalogue of waste. Yet there remains one advantage: this closed world of wrecked ships provides historians with information about the people who built them and died in them. The late twentieth century has increasingly wonderful means of exploiting this and can come to conclusions with consummate accuracy.

With the rise of the twentieth-century fishing industry in the north-west, trawler incidents took precedence. The human and abiding interest these particular vessels arouse, especially now that the industry is in decline, deserves a book to itself, so we will not be concerned with trawler wrecks here.

By the late 1920s and onwards there were other kinds of wrecks, but thankfully they were few. Fred Atherton, master of the *Aquilla* of Liverpool, No.124059, a 172-ton steel fore and aft schooner owned by the Zillah Shipping Carrying Co., made a statement on oath that on 12 January 1925 his ship was proceeding from Belfast to

Peel on the flood tide with a strong wind blowing from the south. On the 13th they were forced to put into Ramsey Bay to clear the engine room pumps which had become choked. A moderate wind increased to gale force and by 11.30 p.m. the chief engineer reported pumps choked again and fires going out owing to stokehold plates and platform being displaced with water. Flares were sent up immediately for assistance, and at 12.30 a.m. the steam trawler *Lena Melling* took the *Aquilla* in tow. This casualty involved no loss of life. Built of steel at Troon in 1907, the *Aquilla* was classed A1 at Lloyds.

Three miles north of Wyre Light, on Christmas Day 1929, the 6,000-ton liner *Tchad* was on her last voyage to the breaker's yard when she dragged anchor not far from Heysham. In order to attract attention on shore, the captain ordered all the mattresses to be burned. Festive season or not, when the maroons were heard the town of Fleetwood turned out in force. From all directions, streets rang to the clatter of clogged feet. As for the lifeboat, there were more volunteers than places. Fourteen men with their Sunday-best clothes under cork jackets and oilskins left the Christmas feasting to set off in rescue of the crew of the *Tchad*. It took two hours to come alongside and get the men to safety.

On 7 October 1931 the yacht *Lady Anne* set sail from Barrow to return to her homeport of Fleetwood and created a mystery which to this day remains unsolved.

The Lytham lifeboat in 1936 after a practice launch.

Laying a sewage pipe in the summer of 1981, the Holland dredger came to grief in an unexpected storm.

Originally a 30ft prawner designed for use in the shallow, stormy, tricky waters of Morecambe Bay, she was built in 1904 by Crosfields of Arnside for William Hornby, subsequently being taken over for racing by Charles Tatham, a well-known local yachtsman.

In the 1928 annual race to the Isle of Man she swooped in like a bird, taking second place. Again and again she proved herself capable of coping with the capricious Irish Sea.

On that unforgettable voyage in 1931 Paul was joined by his cousin Alan, a solicitor, and by two other family connections: a twenty-three-year-old man named Hugan, on leave from the Merchant Navy, and seventeen-year-old Timothy Swarbrick from Wardleys, where *Lady Anne* was usually moored. All were experienced yachtsmen.

At about 9 a.m. *Lady Anne* had left Fleetwood for Barrow where, fed and refreshed, the party of four completed their business. Four hours later *Lady Anne* sailed herself up the River Wyre as though knowing her way. Turning at Wyre Light, she fouled no buoys and sped down channel to ground eventually alongside Fleetwood Pier. She was observed gliding flawlessly downriver, completing the trip, but not one of the crew was found to be aboard, nor were they ever seen again.

Though her sails were set, the vessel was, upon investigation, found to be partially disabled. The yachtsmen had been seen to commence their homeward journey in

The old wooden lifeboat house at Fleetwood in a rough sea, 1936, showing one of the ornamental cannon that were situated on Fleetwood's sea front until they went for the War Effort in 1943. The lifeboat house was demolished in 1976 and its records placed in Fleetwood Museum.

The *Allandale* turned over and sank at North End in the early morning of 4 February 1959. Owned by R. Abel & Sons, Liverpool, the salvage vessel *Topmast 16* (Risdon-Beazley, Southampton) was used to salvage her from the Wyre.

the 7-ton cutter at about 2.30 p.m. Piel lifeboatmen, out for practice, saw *Lady Anne* making for Lune Deeps. All seemed to be well. The next to see her were the keepers on Wyre Light. Noticing she was unmanned, they flew distress signals to warn those on shore. The steam trawler *Agnes Wickfield*, coasting down channel, saw *Lady Anne*'s masthead was broken and her sails displaced. The trawler drew alongside, but her crew's shouts were met with silence. News spread fast and hundreds of people visited the spot near the pier guarded by police. Men worked till midnight dismantling *Lady Anne* by the light of lamps. The mast, with its trailing gear and sails, was first unstepped and the boat fittings removed. The fathers of Hughan and Swarbrick stood by with other relatives, hoping that somewhere, somehow, survivors had been picked up, but first light of morning broke with no news.

Local seafarers, men with a lifetime's experience of Danger Patch near Lune Deeps, talked of a deadly characteristic presented by Fisher's Brow Patches, a shallow stretch where the water suddenly varied from twenty-three fathoms to seven. At exceptionally low tides such as that October's, sudden bad weather could create danger. In such a heavy swell as was running that Wednesday afternoon the yacht could have bumped at this point, flinging out all the occupants. But at no time could the wind be said to have been dangerous to men experienced in handling yachts. The short squall that had sprung up was well within their capabilities and *Lady Anne*'s seaworthiness. 'Something terrible must have happened, and not far from the mouth of the Wyre', said C.E. Tatham, the previous owner. 'Two years ago I sailed her in the Fleetwood to Ramsey race and she was the only boat to finish. There were heavy seas on that occasion'.

A workman on the sea defences, G, Skeogh, reported sighting *Lady Anne* at 4 p.m. making for the light, struggling but keeping her course, turning well with the current as though being properly handled, then beaching herself between the pier and the piles. 'When I saw her she seemed to be answering to someone at the helm and she did that all the way. I saw nothing of men being thrown out near Wyre Light. It was uncanny. Had she been steered, she could not have been kept on a better course'.

Further examination showed that there were no scratches on her to prove that she had struck the bottom. What little underwater damage there was had been done as she lay off Fleetwood Pier.

Barrow seamen, equally experienced, believed that *Lady Anne* was over-canvassed when she set out, sailing with a slack mainshaft. Months later the men who did the repairs at Barrow reported that the main sheet was bent backwards as though tremendous strain had been put upon it. They believed that *Lady Anne*, sailing at speed, had fouled some object with such resultant force that all four crew were flung into the water and drowned. But that did not explain why no bodies were recovered, or how *Lady Anne* managed to sail on for home with such aplomb, as though still in skilled hands.

In January 1936 a 200-ton Manx coaster, *Bradda*, capsized off the Crosby lightship in a gale with only one survivor who swam ashore after displaying great heroism. Five men vanished under the waves. May 1938 brought news that *Lost Horizon* (the barquentine *Emily Warbriek* fitted out as a yacht with diesel engines) had caught fire returning from the West Indies. A Swedish steamer took off the crew and 'old Emily' was abandoned on the high seas.

The whole world waited in 1939 as ninety-nine men died slowly, trapped in the submarine *Thetis* in Liverpool Bay. The third of the new T-class submarines ordered for the Royal Navy in 1936, she left the Birkenhead yards of Cammell Laird on 1 June with 103 naval and civilian personnel. Her escort was the Liverpool tug *Grebecock* with a young naval telegraphist aboard who had not been happy about the way *Thetis* dived.

'What was the duration of Thetis dive?' This question, crackling over the ether, was overlaid with the first warning that all was not well, for it had taken fifty-eight minutes to overcome buoyancy, followed by a sudden plunge below the surface. Frustration and anxiety increased, as there was doubt as to the precise diving position. In failing light the distress buoy released by *Thetis* was finally spotted by an RAF Anson, but the submarine was not found until 7.50 a.m. by the destroyer HMS *Brazen*, who reported part of the stern protruding from the sea.

Captain H. Oram and Lt. F. Woods were chosen to try to reach the surface in order to explain the failing and to help organise the rescue. Both were picked up, but the men inside the submarine were so weakened by carbon monoxide poisoning that they had difficulty in using the escape equipment, and only two more got away. Meanwhile the wire rope connected to the *Thetis* snapped with the rising tides. It was a disaster of heart-breaking proportions, keenly felt in the north-west.

Half covered by the tide, the dredger *Astland*, holed when she ran aground in the channel at Lytham, 17 January 1961, is examined by divers while a boat passes in the background.

In June 1955 *Mona's Isle* was in collision with the inshore fishing boat *Ludo* in the River Wyre. The one-armed owner of the *Ludo*, Hugh Francis Stewart, lost his life. It was very dark with a strong ebb tide running, which got hold of the ship. For a time there was grave risk to her and her passengers, the Masters of the Manx boat being faced with an agonising decision involving ship, passengers and two fishermen in the water.

Moby Dick, a Morecambe tourist attraction, was destroyed by fire in the flaming June of 1970. Launched at Glasson Dock in 1887, her original name was *Ryelands*.

Faroese schooner *Stella Marie*, wrecked off Fleetwood with a cargo of fish.

In October 1939 a steamer *Pegu* was wrecked off Formby. She was a Henderson liner of Glasgow which went to pieces in heavy seas. The New Brighton lifeboat saved passengers and crew and in the same month, also off Formby, was stranded *Ionic Star*, built in 1917, breaking her back and becoming a total loss.

A terrific gale on 25 November 1939 drove the 433-ton pilot boat *Charles Livingston* ashore at Ainsdale Beach on waves 20ft high. The Lytham and Blackpool lifeboats reached the stranded steamer, the Blackpool boat taking off ten survivors. Twenty-three lives were lost. Her master thought she had beached in North Wales and fruitless hours of search were spent in the wrong area.

Had it not been wartime, the disaster might never have happened. Early in the morning of Sunday 26 November 1939, Southport was completely blacked out. On one of the worst storms for years, all taking place in pitch darkness, it must have been an appalling experience. Some of the men leapt overboard and swam in the wrong direction, only to drown. Most were washed exhausted and helpless off the deck or rigging to which they were clinging, 500 yards from the shore. By dusk that same evening thousands of people, drawn by the timeless fascination of wreck-gazing, braved the gale, walking up to the *Charles Livingston*, left high and dry by the receding tide. Of eleven pilots who had been on board, only four survived. The six men in the rigging, Pilot Ronald Patterson of Thornton amongst them, had been there for eight hours whilst the whole of the boat, apart from mast and rigging, was in the surging sea. It is interesting to note that the survivors lashed themselves to the rigging in the manner of sailors 100 years before them. All the bodies were washed up within a mile of the wreck, apart from that of Albert Jones, second engineer, who was found on 3 December on the Horse Bank.

One of the last great wartime lifeboat rescues off Fleetwood was in October 1941 when the schooner *Stella Marie*, travelling from the Faroes to Fleetwood, anchored four miles out near North Wharf in worsening weather. Efforts to reach harbour were hampered by cable parting and anchor fouling. The drifting schooner accepted the offer of a tow but ill luck persisted. With the hawser breaking and the weather rapidly becoming atrocious, *Stella Marie* was seen to be in such danger that the Fleetwood lifeboat ventured on one of the most difficult rescues in its career. The eight-man crew of the *Stella Marie* were in the rigging when, after ploughing through heavy seas, the lifeboat hove to under Coxswain Jeff Wright. Again and again pounding waves and surf completely submerged and hurled the lifeboat against the stricken schooner, which caused the steel pintle of the lifeboat rudder to bend and jam. Brave, determined efforts were eventually rewarded and all eight men rescued. Jeff Wright and Mechanic Sid Hill were awarded RNLI silver medals engraved 'Let not the deep swallow them up'. Monetary awards and vellum inscriptions were presented to other members of the crew. In summer months the wreck is still visible and the blonde-coloured pitch pine of the decks has been reported still bright under its coating of green moss. Over the past forty years a girdle of gravel has built up round the wreck which is occasionally visited by 'wreck trekkers', but it is an unwise thing to do as sea mists can swoop down like steam from a giant kettle without any warning.

Another wreck, the *Zion Hill*, once a favourite to visit, was carrying tons of concrete when she broke her back on an ebbing tide, caught upon what some people insist are the remnants of Portus Setantiorum, a harbour constructed in Roman times. When this clay and boulder embankment is visible, masters of the Manx boats are warned not to attempt to enter the Channel. Some believe it to be a terminal moraine from a glacial age, but as the Romans were great colonisers and the sea has eaten away two and a half miles of coastline since their day, the protagonists could be right, especially as old salts for more than a century have called the place 'Roman Harbour'.

The *Zion Hill* was a schooner of 114 tons from Portmadoc, commanded by Captain D. Davies. She was travelling at the time (December 1877) from London to Lancaster, a succession of gales having forced her to shelter at several points and prolonged her voyage to three weeks. A solitary Fleetwood spectator apparently ran round the town shouting 'Man the lifeboat', and such haste was made that the *Edward Wasey* was launched without first removing the carriage. The same resourceful character dived to cut the ropes which held her fast, but the tragi-comedy did not end there, for the six men of *Zion Hill*, after fighting desperately to save the vessel, had to take to their small boat. Whilst rowing towards Fleetwood they had been passed by the eager *Edward Wasey*, their shouts to attract attention going unheard. It was a wild night with strong tides, but fortunately no loss of life. At the lowest tides of the year the *Zion Hill*'s remains were easily located by the bags of cement that had set in weird shapes through which large sea eels swam in and out. Enthusiasts usually came back with a bag of eels to make into the local delicacy, eel pie, dressed with pickled samphire.

On 13 March 1940 the 500-ton motor vessel *Union*, a Dutch coaster, came aground opposite the Palace Hotel, Southport, mistaking a set of flashing lights. She was registered at Groningen from Amsterdam and fortunately re-floated on the next tide with but slight damage. In September 1950 the schooner *Happy Harry*, a three-masted vessel, broke in a gale off Crosby, the crew being taken off by the New Brighton lifeboat. The vessel finally dragged its anchors and crashed into the pier.

Glasson Dock. The *Moby Dick* became a show ship, used in the film of the same name about the white whale and Captain Ahab.

During the third week in January 1954, Fleetwood lifeboat was launched for the second time in seven days, and, following a seven-hour voyage in gales, she spent sixteen hours in blinding snowstorms in one of the greatest combined searches ever made in Morecambe Bay. But it was all in vain. Not a ship but an RAF Wellington bomber had sent out the distress call, 'Icing up, baling out'. Despite the efforts of six lifeboats, trawlers, naval ships and aircraft, no sign of survivors or wreckage was found.

The lifeboat crew made the longest trip on local record, going out without food, sustained only by emergency rations of self-heating tins of soup and cocoa, chocolate biscuits and bottles of rum. Yet they were ready to go back again within an hour of the boat returning (after using 100 gallons, it ran out of petrol). However, with the bitterly cold conditions hope had faded and the order was for them to stand by as planes continued their fruitless search throughout the night.

The heat wave summer of June 1970 led to the burning of the *Moby Dick* in one of the worst days of fire Morecambe had ever known. The Alhambra Theatre and the old film-set schooner, such an attraction for visitors, went up in smoke within minutes of each other. Tinder-dry, the schooner, originally called *Ryelands*, was launched in 1887 at Glasson, and after a useful life at sea, was more recently used in the making of films *Moby Dick*, *Treasure Island* and *Frenchman's Creek*.

How many craft, one wonders, met their doom before records were kept? In 200 years more than 300 vessels came to grief on the sandbanks of the Mersey Estuary, between Waterloo and Ribble. The Horse Bank has already been referred to as a graveyard of ships. Since the longships of the Norsemen and the galleys of the Romans, racing currents and shifting banks ceaselessly carry on their business of burying. Sometimes when gales spring up aided by mountainous, scouring seas, for a time the sands reveal some of their secrets. In 1974 the keel of a wooden schooner was flung onto the Formby beach, another at Cleveleys in 1966 (my young son wanted to tow it home behind the car!). Local fishermen have tales of wrecks appearing between tides only to be buried again in the continuing turbulence, before ever their presence can be charted.

What appeared to be the truck or circular platform of a masted Elizabethan ship was at one time visible at low water in the Freshfield area and known as Barnacle Bill.

Wrecks coming and going according to the wind and the listing of the tide are, of course, a problem to coastguards and a hazard to shipping. For weeks in 1920, intermittently and without warning, dogs howled, residents grumbled, houses shook to their foundations at reverberating attempts to blow up wrecks off the north-west coast. As recently as 1978 the firm of John N. Ward came up against the problem of finding the owner of the *Albany*, wrecked seventy years before. A salvaging company, Mull of Kintyre Divers, wished to buy her. But that is another story, close to our own times and most interesting of all, perhaps, concerning trawlers and trawlermen, a breed living 'a life apart', with that instinct all seamen have – plus something extra.

Jacinta FD 159, built in 1972.

Jacinta

Jacinta FD 159, built in 1972.

Of all fishing vessels, *Jacinta* is classed the most famous. There have been three *Jacinta*s. The first, FD 235, was a coal-fired trawler launched in 1915. It was she who joined the flotilla led by trawler *Gava*, FD 380, and like *Gava* she performed bravely at Dunkirk, embarking 150 French troops.

The second *Jacinta*, FD 21, now diesel-powered, appeared in 1955. She was scrapped in 1971.

The third *Jacinta*, pictured here, is a stern trawler. Now restored and preserved for posterity, she proved to be a record breaker (top earning trawler). But she has known grim times in deep waters, facing many a storm. In 1982 she had a historic trip, coming to port with her last major haul of fish and the following day, to the sound of the traditional lament, sailing for Hull. She was the largest trawler in J. Marr & Sons middle-water fleet.

Riverdance

There can be few things more exciting to a local historian than to feel they are living in the presence of history. So I thought one particularly stormy night, 31 January 2008. It was pitch dark outside and the wind howled.

The news of a sea drama, unfolding whilst I was scribbling away about the wreck of the *Abana* in 1894, was very exciting. What's that? It is all happening on much the same spot! Yet another victim of the Irish Sea's fury, just fields away from my house, was being battered by giant waves.

Along with the TV newscaster's words, stark, live, pictorial coverage was flickering from the small screen telling the country that in severe storm conditions a freak wave had caused the Irish ferry ship *Riverdance* to move so erratically that containers had toppled, some even breaking loose. Result? *Riverdance* was listing heavily at the mercy of the Irish Sea, that graveyard of ships. Gales of over 70mph were

Riverdance with some of the ribs of the *Abana*, wrecked in 1894, in the foreground. Hopeful beachcombers with metal detectors still circle the remains of the *Abana*.

The Abana Bell.

In the early hours of 22nd December 1894, in a great gale, the 1200 ton timber ship Abana foundered off the coast at Little Bispham and at ebb-tide the ship's ribs are still to be seen in the sand. The alarm was raised by Robert Hindle of the Cleveleys Hotel, & the 16 members of the crew, who were all saved by the Blackpool Life-boat, presented him with the ship's bell. Abana was built in New Brunswick, Canada, in 1874, & her bell bears a record of this.--- At the turn of the century a number of Cleveleys people began working for a Parish Church. After meeting above the Rossall Road Post Office, regular services were held in the Institute which was near the present Bus Station. Mr & Mrs. Hindle, members of this group, presented the Bell to the church, where it was rung each Sunday to call the faithful to worship, until St. Andrew's Church was built in 1910. For years Abana Bell aroused little interest except in local historians, but now the new North west porch of the Church, built 1976, affords it a suitable setting. It will be rung again at every service for the interment of ashes in the Garden of Remembrance.

Left: Citation. The *Abana.*

Below: Riverdance.

making rescue operations so dangerous as to be impossible. Weather was being described as 'horrendous' and Fylde folks in their snug centrally heated houses knew that well, as the wind's screeching crescendo made doors rattle and wheelie bins topple like ships' containers.

From as far away as Anglesey helicopters managed to effect a magnificent rescue of twenty-three passengers and crew. All had to be winched off in appalling conditions, which demanded bravery of the highest order. All hope of securing cargo was abandoned. Lorry driver Nigel Bucknall managed to call his wife by mobile phone from the deck of the stricken ferry, saying 'Mary, I love you', admitting later that he feared he would never see her again. Amidst the din of Nature's anger and a reeling vessel, it must have been terrifying.

On that storm-tossed night events unfolded as follows:

1.45 p.m. The captain of the *Riverdance* issued his mayday call, 'Ship listing badly after being hit by huge wave.'

8 p.m. RAF helicopter crews on standby and by 8.20 p.m. they had scrambled to the scene. Fleetwood and Lytham lifeboats had already been launched and were ploughing through the mountainous seas.

9 p.m. Passengers and crew assembled on ship's deck as operations to winch them to safety began.

11.45 p.m. *Riverdance* reported firmly aground off Anchorsholme.

By 3 a.m. the ship's master decided to wait for high tide in a bid to re-float the vessel, but by 5.20 a.m. the last nine remaining crew were air lifted off the vessel, which every effort had failed to re-float.

By early next morning, with the gale still so strong you could lean on it, thousands of sightseers had gathered on the cliffs and the shore to gaze in awe at this incredible hulk, naked, the tide having receded and the ship leaning at what seemed an ever-increasing angle.

Foolhardy seekers after loot had to be severely warned to stay clear as the situation was potentially dangerous, but in the months ahead *Riverdance* was to prove one of the biggest crowd pullers since the days when Horatio Nelson's flagship, the *Foudroyant*, was dashed to pieces off North Pier, Blackpool.

In their thousands they came from all over the country, and local shopkeepers rejoiced. Crowds helped to fill failing tills of local tradespeople, who, one year on are still marvelling at the sudden 'corn in Egypt' brought by a wreck – lucky for some! *Riverdance* proved to be a massive tourist attraction, the kind that Blackpool gloried in, but she was to

Above and below: The Irish ferry was wrecked on 31 January 2008. The actual place of grounding for the *Riverdance* was Anchorsholme, Norbreck (not Blackpool), near to where the *Abana* grounded and broke up in December 1894.

Riverdance lies exposed.

prove difficult to move. From 31 January onwards, *Riverdance* acted like a magnet and the country's press headed towards the monster, beached so ingloriously.

It took almost ten months to completely remove the remains. The wreck could not be re-floated but had to be drained of environmentally hazardous oil. The Maritime & Coastguard Agency decreed she must be cut away in small sections and carried away.

Although the vessel never tipped fully on her side, thousands of pounds of stock washed ashore. Bags of peat and compost and sodden chocolate biscuits littered the sandy site. Fortunately there was nothing dangerously pollutant. Surefreight had six trucks on the *Riverdance* carrying timber and recycled paper bound for Heysham and Fleetwood, and Vincent Waddell was sure the stranding would cost his firm at least £10,000, but there was much more to consider – trade routes shut down, the backlog was a headache – but shopkeepers are still talking of 'the dizzy heights' of sales brought by that lumbering wayward giant, *Riverdance*.

Crowds gather to watch the *Riverdance*.

The sea reclaims the wreck.

Appendix I

Masted Barques

The four-masted barque was one of the original rigs of the big sea-going sailing ships. A barque is a vessel of three or more masts, square-rigged on all except the 'aftermast', which is fore and aft rigged.

At one time it became impossible and uneconomical to use the full-rigged ship. Crews had to be economised and so the four-master became the favourite. The masts were named Fore, Main, Mizzen and Jigger. This four-masted barque is illustrated on an old Wills's Cigarette card, shown under 'plain sail and close hauled', which means her yards are braced up to bring about sailing as near as possible to the wind. (This of course was not possible in storm and tempest.) Then sails must be hauled in before the wind turned to gale, which could tear them away from the masts.

A cigarette card from the late Mr Tom Pocock's collection.

Appendix II

Nautical Terms

In the days of the sailing ships, William Spavens, in his *Memories of a sea-faring life*, explained over 400 nautical terms. This was in the 1790s. I name but a few:

Abaft – towards the stern
Afore – forward
Aloft – top of the mast-head
Avast – stop!
Bonnet – a piece of canvas to mend a sail
Yards – spars of wood on which the sails are set
Cringle – a hole in a sail
Hawser – a small cable to use with a kedge anchor (see illustration – the kedge anchor could be vital in saving a wrecked ship).

But of all 400, I liked 'Burgoo', meaning porridge, the best. These terms were current in Spavens' day; and more have been added or abridged since.

lmirante Saldana, 1933. A four-masted barquentine, a steel craft used as a ship for crew training. She had a spread of 27,000sq.ft of canvas.